D0442791

ACCELERATE

JOHN P. KOTTER

ACCELERATE

BUILDING STRATEGIC AGILITY FOR A FASTER-MOVING WORLD

Harvard Business Review Press
Boston, Massachusetts

Copyright © 2014 John P. Kotter
All rights reserved
Printed in the United States of America

10 9 8 7 6 5 4 3 2 1

No part of this publication may be reproduced, stored in or introduced into
a retrieval system, or transmitted, in any form, or by any means (electronic,
mechanical, photocopying, recording, or otherwise), without the prior
permission of the publisher. Requests for permission should be directed to
permissions@hbsp.harvard.edu, or mailed to Permissions, Harvard Business School Publishing, 60 Harvard Way, Boston, Massachusetts 02163.

The web addresses referenced in this book were live and correct at the time
of the book's publication but may be subject to change.

Library of Congress Cataloging-in-Publication Data

Kotter, John P., 1947–
    Accelerate : building strategic agility for a faster-moving world /
John P. Kotter.
        pages   cm
    ISBN 978-1-62527-174-7 (alk. paper)
    1. Organizational change.   2. Strategic planning.   3. Management.
I. Title.
    HD58.8.K6447   2014
    658.4′012—dc23   2013050671

eISBN: 9781625272546

The paper used in this publication meets the requirements of the American National Standard for Permanence of Paper for Publications and
Documents in Libraries and Archives Z39.48-1992.

CONTENTS

PREFACE

We are crossing a line into a territory with unpredictable turmoil and exponentially growing change—change for which we are not prepared. Here I describe what some pioneers have successfully done to win, and win big, in this emerging environment.

Accelerate is about how to handle strategic challenges fast enough, with agility and creativity, to take advantage of windows of opportunity which open and shut more quickly today. It shows how people in some leading, innovative organizations move ahead of fierce competition, deal with unprecedented turmoil, and cope with the constant threat of technological discontinuities—all without sacrificing short-term results or wearing out their workforces.

My conclusions as presented here are fundamental. The world is now changing at a rate at which the basic systems, structures, and cultures built over the past century cannot keep up with the demands being placed on them. Incremental adjustments to how you manage and strategize, no matter how clever, are not up to the job. You need something very new to stay ahead in an age of tumultuous change and growing uncertainties.

The solution is not to trash what we know and start over but instead to reintroduce, in an organic way, a second system—one which would be familiar to most successful entrepreneurs. The new system adds needed agility and speed while the old one, which keeps running, provides reliability and efficiency. The two together—a dual system—are actually very similar to what all mature organizations had at one point in their life cycles, yet did not sustain (and have long since forgotten). There is a practical way to create this dual operating system, and it can be done very inexpensively. Results come quickly. I have seen people do it. It works.

The origins of this project build on previous research I have done on large-scale change: work funded by the Harvard Business School, where I have been teaching for many decades. A report on that research was first published in my book *Leading Change* (1996) and extended with follow-up reports in *The Heart of Change* (2002), *Our Iceberg Is Melting* (2006), *A Sense of Urgency* (2008), and *Buy-in* (2010). That work, in turn, was built on my early examinations of leadership, which go all the way back to 1974, with perhaps the most important report on that subject published in 1990 as *A Force for Change: How Leadership Is Different from Management*. I am sometimes amazed at how robust the conclusions from these studies remain today—how they still speak to us even though the world facing business leaders (and those in government, the nonprofit sector, and education) has changed so much. What I present in this book adds to my prior work. This is not a case in which new realities mean that old ideas are no longer valid. It is more a case of adding to previous conclusions in a way that takes us to some very big new ideas.

Up until this project, all of my past work, research now spanning many decades, has used the same formula. Find cases representing the highest 10% or 20% of performers. Observe what they do. Talk to people who have lived in those situations. Then do the same for the average performers and for the laggards. Look for patterns that show the differences. Report those patterns with an emphasis on factors that you can change—to take average performance to high or lagging results at least up to the norm.

With this project, for the first time in my career, I have tried a formula that is different in two fundamental ways. Here I begin by looking at people truly pushing the envelope. I mean only the top 1% or so—those who have achieved extraordinary successes through very new ways of operating. Then I watch as others (usually with the assistance of the Kotter International consulting group) try to replicate the very best, in their own way, in their own industries or organizations. This shift feels sort of like going from basic research in a pharmaceutical firm to basic research plus product development plus clinical trials.

Accelerate is for leaders willing and able to see the stark realities of today's business environment, to know that bold change is necessary, and to take the journey, to blaze the trail. I hope the stories here of early, successful pioneers will affirm your own decisions in this direction, give you the confidence to go further, and inspire much-needed additional action. There is no question in my mind that much more is required in order to build organizations that win today and will win again in the future. Much more is needed to build thriving economies that can help pull billions of people on this small planet up to a better, more prosperous place.

This effort has been formally funded by Kotter International, where I serve as the director of research and which helps pioneers do what I write about in this book. Informally, Harvard continues to be of great assistance, no longer through funding but most certainly through comments on drafts of books from executive students and faculty colleagues.

As always, many specific people share some credit for this work. They include, particularly, Dennis Goin and Randy Ottinger from Kotter International, and Amy Bernstein and Jeff Kehoe from Harvard Business Publishing.

ACCELERATE

ONE

LIMITS OF HIERARCHY IN A FASTER-MOVING WORLD

This is a book about pioneers, for pioneers.

The topics I address here are associated with a single game-changing observation: organizations everywhere are struggling to keep up with the accelerating pace of change—let alone get ahead of it.

Most people don't feel the full rush going on around them, which is a part of the problem. But objectively, the data are convincing. On almost every important business index, the world is racing ahead. The stakes— the financial, social, environmental, and political consequences—are rising in a similar exponential way.

In this new world, the big question facing business leaders everywhere is how to stay competitive and grow profitably amid this increasing turbulence and disruption. The most fundamental problem is that any company that has made it past the start-up stage is optimized

No matter how you look at it, the world is moving faster

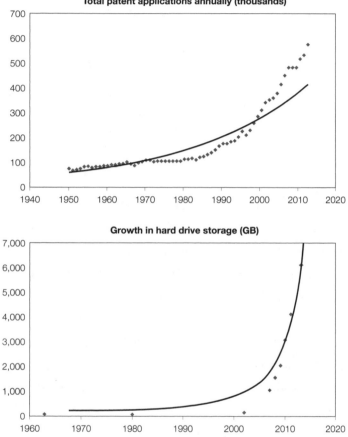

Sources: US Patent and Trademark Office (patents filed), multiple news reports and data files (hard drive storage).

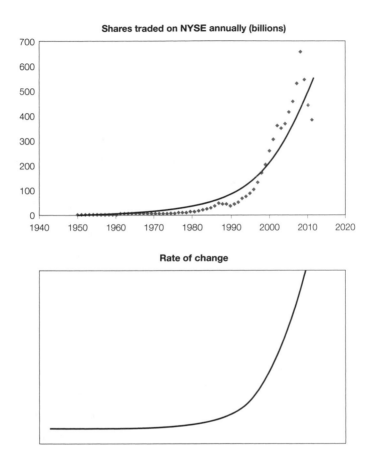

Source: New York Stock Exchange (volume of shares traded).

much more for efficiency than for strategic agility—the ability to capitalize on opportunities and dodge threats with speed and assurance. I could give you a hundred examples of companies that, like Borders and Research in Motion (RIM), recognized the need for a big strategic move but couldn't pull themselves together fast enough to make it and ended up sitting on the sidelines as nimbler competitors beat them, badly. The examples always play out the same way: an organization that's suddenly facing a real threat or eyeing a Big Opportunity tries—and fails—to cram through significant changes using structures, processes, and methods that worked well in the past. But the old ways of setting and executing new strategies are failing us.

Companies used to reconsider their basic strategies only rarely, when they were forced to do so. Today any company that isn't rethinking its direction at least every few years (as well as constantly adjusting to shifting contexts) and then quickly making necessary operational changes is putting itself at risk. That's what a faster-moving world is doing to us. But as any business leader can attest, the tension between what it takes to stay ahead of increasingly fierce competition, on the one hand, and needing to deliver this year's results, on the other, can be overwhelming.

We cannot discount the daily demands of running a company, which traditional hierarchies and managerial processes can still do very well. What they do *not* do well is identify the most important hazards or opportunities early enough, formulate innovative strategic initiatives nimbly enough, and (especially) execute those initiatives fast enough.

FROM NETWORKS TO HIERARCHIES

Virtually all successful organizations on earth go through a very similar life cycle. They begin with a network-like structure, sort of like a solar system with a sun, planets, moons, and even satellites. Founders are at the center. Others are at various nodes working on different initiatives. Action is opportunity seeking and risk taking, all guided by a vision that people buy into. Energized individuals move quickly and with agility.

Over time, a successful organization evolves through a series of stages (more on that later, because it is important) into an enterprise that is structured as a hierarchy and is driven by well-known managerial processes: planning, budgeting, job defining, staffing, measuring, problem solving. With a well-structured hierarchy and with managerial processes that are driven with skill, this

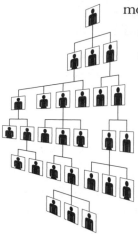 more mature organization can produce incredibly reliable and efficient results on a weekly, quarterly, and annual basis.

A well-designed hierarchy allows us to sort work into departments, product divisions, and regions, where strong expertise is developed and nurtured, time-tested procedures are invented and used, and there are clear reporting relationships and accountability. Couple that with managerial processes that can guide and coordinate the actions of employees—even thousands of employees located around the globe—and such an operating system lets people do what they know how to do exceptionally well.

There are those who deride all of this as a bureaucratic leftover from the past, not fit to handle twenty-first-century needs. Get rid of it. Smash it. Start over. Organize as a spider web. Eliminate middle management and let the staff manage themselves. But the truth is that the management-driven hierarchies which good enterprises use and we take for granted are one of the most amazing innovations of the twentieth century. And they are still absolutely necessary to make organizations work.

One part of what makes them amazing is that they can be enhanced to deal with change, going beyond mere repetition—at least up to a point. We have learned how to launch initiatives within a hierarchical system to take on new tasks and improve performance on old ones. We know how to identify new problems, find and analyze data in a dynamic marketplace, and build business cases for changing what we make, how we make it, how we sell it, and where we sell it. We've learned how to execute these changes by adding task forces, tiger teams, project management departments, and executive sponsors for new initiatives. We can do this while still taking care of the day-to-day work of the organization because this strategic change methodology is easily accommodated by a hierarchical structure and basic managerial processes. And that is precisely what leaders everywhere have been doing, and to a greater degree, each year.

Every relevant survey of executives I have seen for a decade now reports that they are launching more strategic initiatives than ever. Skilled leaders have always tried to improve productivity, but now they are trying to innovate more and faster. When historical organizational cultures—formed over many years or decades—have slowed action, impatient leaders are trying to change those cultures. The goal of all this, of course, is to accelerate profitable growth to keep up or get ahead of the competition.

But those same surveys show that success across these initiatives is often illusive. A recent reboot at JCPenney, for example, looked exceptionally promising—for a few months. And then all the various strategic projects began to fall apart.

THE LIMITS OF MANAGEMENT-DRIVEN HIERARCHIES

The frustrations of this reality are well known.

You find yourself going back again and again to the same small number of trusted people to lead key initiatives. That puts obvious limits on what can be done and at what speed.

You find that communication across silos does not happen with sufficient speed and effectiveness. The same is true of information flowing from the top of the organization to the bottom and from the bottom up. Net result: more stalling.

You find that policies, rules, and procedures, even sensible ones, become barriers to strategic speed. These inevitably grow over time, implemented as solutions to real problems of cost, quality, or compliance. But in a faster-moving world they become, at a minimum, bumps in the road—if not outright cement barriers.

You find that short-term focus on the quarterly numbers clashes with a forward-looking drive to speed ahead of the competition. At a meeting to talk about both a big program to magnify innovation and cleanup efforts after a fire in one of your plants, you know which topic occupies most of the conversation. Multiply this inherent tendency by a hundred or a thousand and it becomes inevitable that so many ideas to boost an organization's capacity to innovate and win will either stall or die.

Part of the problem is political and social: people are often loath to take chances without permission from superiors. Part of it is simply related to human nature: people cling to their habits and fear loss of power and stature.

Complacency and insufficient buy-in, a typical product of past success, complicate matters further. With even a little complacency, people don't believe anything much new is needed and begin to resist change. With insufficient buy-in, they might believe something new is needed, but not the strategic initiatives being launched from the top. Both attitudes stall acceleration.

It can be tempting to simply blame the problems on people: the control-obsessed middle managers or the my-career-first MBA staff. But the reality is that the problem is *systemic* and directly related to the limitations of hierarchy and basic managerial processes.

Silos are an inherent part of hierarchical operating systems. They can be made with thinner walls and leaders can try to make them less parochial, but they cannot be eliminated. So too with rules and procedures: we can reduce their number, but we will always need some of them. The list of similar issues goes on and on. You can reduce but not eliminate levels. You can tell people not to ignore the long term but you cannot eliminate quarterly budgets. These and other factors are an inherent part of the system and, predictably, eventually

Acceleration stalled

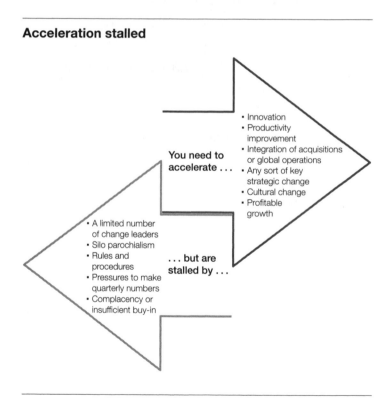

become anchors on efforts to accelerate strategic agility and strategy execution in a faster-moving world.

Good leaders know all these things, if sometimes only intuitively, and try to make up for the problems with those speed-it-up enhancements. They create all sorts of project-management organizations to handle special projects. They use interdepartmental task forces to cut across silos. They bring in strategy consultants or build strategic planning departments to focus on longer-term issues. In a similar way, they add strategic planning to the yearly operational planning exercise. They build in change-management capabilities to overcome complacency, lower resistance, and increase buy-in. When done well, these and other enhancements can reduce the problems with stalling and increase speed and agility—*but only up to a point.*

What we need today is a powerful new element to address the challenges posed by mounting complexity and rapid change. The solution, which I have seen work astonishingly well, is a second system that is organized as a network—more like a start-up's solar system than a mature organization's Giza pyramid—that can create agility and speed. It powerfully complements rather than overburdens a more mature organization's hierarchy, thus freeing the latter to do what it's optimized to do. It makes an enterprise easier to run while accelerating strategic change. This is not a question of "either/or." It's "both/and": two systems that operate in concert. A dual operating system.

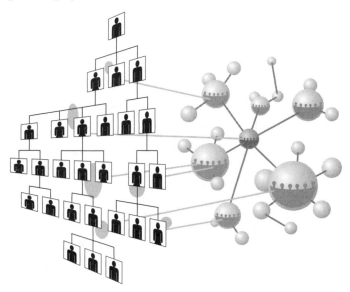

A NEW DIRECTION

Let me be clear. I am not talking about ever more grand interdepartmental task forces, new strategy teams following new models, innovation councils, self-directed work teams, policies that give people time to work on their own creative projects, or all of the above together. These may help movement in the right direction, but they are still just enhancements to a single system. I am talking about a bigger idea, yet one with roots in familiar structures, practices, and thinking.

Most start-ups really are organized as networks because they need to be nimble, swift, and creative in order to grab opportunities. Even in mature organizations, informal networks of change agents frequently operate under the hierarchical radar to make something new happen faster. What I describe here also echoes much of the most interesting management thinking of the past few decades—from Michael Porter's wake-up call telling us that organizations need to pay attention to strategy much more explicitly and frequently, to Clayton Christensen's insights about how poorly companies handle the technological discontinuities inherent in a faster-moving world, to recent work by the Nobel Laureate Daniel Kahneman describing the brain as two coordinated systems, one more emotional and one more rational.

The processes that run within the new network structure look less like systematic management (which creates reliability and efficiency) and more like mobilizing leadership (which creates speed and agility). These processes expand on the eight-step method I first documented fifteen years ago, in my book *Leading Change,* while studying successful large-scale change. The new network part of a dual operating system takes those steps and turbocharges them. It does so by allowing many more people to become active agents of change, who can get more done faster. It does so by building even more powerful strategic urgency—and not just in a general sense but centered around a Big Opportunity. And after starting to deal with a specific strategic challenge, these processes never stop. They become permanent accelerators, creating and maintaining a culture of agility and speed within an organization.

The direction I take in this book—that some pioneers have already taken—solves problems that have been vexing us for decades.

People have been talking for a quarter of a century about the need for more leaders, because in a turbulent world an organization's top two or three executives cannot do it all. But very few jobs in traditional hierarchical organizations provide the information and the experience needed to help people become leaders. And the solutions available—courses on leadership, for example—are obviously inadequate by themselves, because most complex perspectives and skills are developed on the job, not in the classroom.

In the past decade uses of the word "innovation" have multiplied exponentially in reports and conversation. But how many organizations do you know that have innovative finance functions, supply chains, or IT departments? We criticize managers for being dull or shortsighted, but look at the system they live in. Hierarchies with great management processes and good leaders on top are not built for leaping into a creative future. Innovation requires risks, people who are willing to think outside their boxes, perspectives from multiple silos, and more. Management-driven hierarchies are built to minimize risk and keep people in their boxes and silos. To change this more than incrementally is to fight a losing battle.

People have been writing for fifty years about unleashing human potential and passion, then directing the energy to solving significant business challenges. But who, outside the world of start-ups, has succeeded in doing this? So few do because they're working within a system that is designed to get today's job done—a system that asks most people, usually benignly, to be quiet, take orders, and do their jobs in a repetitive way.

People have been grumbling for years about the strategy consulting industry, whose reports often fail to find and (especially) implement strategies to better fit a changing competitive landscape. A consultant's report—all thought and little heart, forecasting where you can flourish in two or five or ten years, produced by smart outsiders, and acted on in a linear way by a limited number of appointed people—has increasingly *less* chance of leading to truly A+ success in a faster-moving and more unpredictable world.

And most fundamentally: For at least twenty years, people have been studying and writing about the increasing speed of business and the need for organizations to be quicker and much more agile. The cries of alarm have grown louder and louder. In one survey of managers and executives by the research unit of the *Financial Times* and a consulting firm, over 90% of the respondents said the importance of "agility and speed has increased in the last five years." When asked "How will your sources of competitive advantage change over the next 15 years?" respondents' number one answer was "Responsiveness to changes in the environment." But who has been able to become truly fast and agile in their response to change, besides a few small high-tech firms? The situation will no longer be improved by tweaking the usual methodology or adding turbochargers to a single hierarchical system. That's like trying to strap a rocket engine onto an elephant so that it can move faster. Good luck.

WHAT NEXT?

So what is ahead? In the next chapter, I will be describing the actual features of a dual operating system, its hierarchy-network structure, the core principles underlying its effectiveness, the Accelerators themselves, and the people who make it all work. Then, in chapter 3, I am going to tell you the story of a firm that shows the stakes involved in operating in a faster-moving world, and how they are much greater than most people can see. In chapter 4, we will explore why today's best practices exist and why they cannot protect us from the downside risks of faster-moving strategic challenges. In chapter 5, we look at how one firm created a dual system and the astonishing business impact it had. Finally, in chapters 6–8 we drill into the details of how firms can get started in creating a dual system.

The remarkable achievements I describe in this book are real—I have not only heard about them but seen them for myself. The pioneers who are doing these things are limited in number now, but they are helping us to understand what is possible and needed. They are mapping what I believe will eventually have to be the future for everyone. We have much to learn from these people, and we should be learning it now.

TWO

SEIZING OPPORTUNITIES WITH A DUAL OPERATING SYSTEM

It seems like new management tools are proposed every week for finding a competitive advantage or dealing with twenty-first-century demands. How is a dual operating system any different? The answer is twofold. First, a dual system is more about *leading* strategic initiatives to capitalize on big opportunities or dodge big threats than it is about management. Second, although the dual system is a new idea, it is a manner of operating that has been hiding in plain sight for years. All successful organizations operate more or less as I describe during the most dynamic growth period in their life cycle. They just don't understand this while it is happening or sustain it as they mature.

A DUAL SYSTEM'S STRUCTURE

The basic structure is self-explanatory: hierarchy on one side and network on the other. The network side mimics successful enterprises in their entrepreneurial phase, before there were organization charts showing reporting relationships, before there were formal job descriptions and status levels. That structure looks roughly like a constantly evolving solar system, with a guiding mechanism as the sun, strategic initiatives as planets, and sub-initiatives as moons or satellites.

This structure is dynamic: initiatives and sub-initiatives coalesce and disband as needed. Although a typical hierarchy tends not to change much from year to year, this type of network typically morphs all the time and with ease. Since it contains no bureaucratic layers, command-and-control prohibitions, and Six Sigma processes, the network permits a level of individualism, creativity, and innovation that even the least bureaucratic hierarchy, 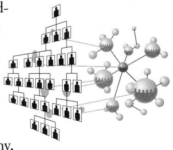 run by the most talented executives, simply cannot provide. Populated with a diagonal slice of employees from all across the organization and up and down its ranks, the network liberates information from silos and hierarchical layers and enables it to flow with far greater freedom and at accelerated speed.

The hierarchy part of the dual operating system differs from almost every other hierarchy today in one very important way. Much of the work ordinarily assigned to it that demands innovation, agility, difficult change, and big strategic initiatives executed quickly—challenges dumped on work streams, tiger teams, or strategy departments—has been shifted over to the network part. That leaves the hierarchy less encumbered and better able to perform what it is designed for: doing today's job well, making incremental changes to further improve efficiency, and handling those strategic initiatives that help a company deal with predictable adjustments, such as routine IT upgrades.

In a truly reliable, efficient, agile, and *fast* enterprise, the network meshes with the more traditional structure; it is not some sort of "super task force" that reports to some level in the hierarchy. It is seamlessly connected to and coordinated with the hierarchy in a number of ways, chiefly through the people who populate both systems. Still, the organization's top management plays a crucial role in starting and maintaining the network. The C-suite or executive committee must launch it, explicitly bless it, support it, and ensure that it and the hierarchy stay aligned. The hierarchy's leadership team must serve as role models for their subordinates in interacting with the network. I have found that none of this requires much C-suite time. But these actions by senior executives clearly signal that the network is not in any way a rogue operation. It is not an informal organization. It is not just a small engagement exercise which makes those who participate feel good. It is part of a system designed for competing and winning.

I am not describing a purely theoretical idea. Every successful organization goes through a phase, usually very early in its history, in which it actually operates with this dual structure (more on that in chapter 4). This is true whether you are Panasonic in Osaka, Morgan Stanley in New York, or a nonprofit in London. The problem is that the network side of a dual system in the normal life cycle of organizations is informal and invisible to most people, so it rarely sustains itself. As they mature, organizations evolve naturally toward a single system—a hierarchical organization—at the expense of the entrepreneurial network. The lack of insight and effort to formalize and sustain an organization that was both highly reliable and efficient on the one hand and fast and agile on the other did not cost us much in a slower moving past. That situation has changed forever—for Panasonic, Morgan Stanley, and thousands of others—or it will soon.

A DUAL OPERATING
SYSTEM'S PRINCIPLES

On close observation, it's clear that a well-functioning dual operating system is guided by a few basic principles:

- **Many people driving important change, and from everywhere, not just the usual few appointees.** It all starts here. For speed and agility, you need a fundamentally different way to gather information, make decisions, and implement decisions that have some strategic significance. You need more eyes to see, more brains to think, and more legs to act in order to accelerate. You need additional people, with their own particular windows on the world and with their additional good working relationships with others, in order to truly innovate. More people need to be able to have the latitude to initiate—not just carry out someone else's directives. But this must be done with proven processes that do not risk chaos, create destructive conflict, duplicate efforts, or waste money. And it must be done with insiders. Two hundred consultants, no matter how smart or dynamic, cannot do the job.

- **A "get-to" mindset, not a "have-to" one.** Every great leader throughout history has demonstrated that it is possible to find many change agents, and from every corner of society—but only if people are given a choice and feel they truly have permission to step forward and act. The desire to work with others for an important and exciting shared purpose, and the realistic possibility of doing so, are key. They always have been. And people who feel they have the privilege of being involved in an important activity have also shown, throughout history, that they will volunteer to do so in addition to their normal activities. You don't have to hire a new crew at great expense. Existing people provide the energy.

- **Action that is head and heart driven, not just head driven.** Most people won't want to help if you appeal only to logic, with numbers and business cases. You must also appeal to how people feel. As have all the great leaders throughout history, you must speak to the genuine and fundamental human desire to contribute to some bigger cause, to take a community or an organization into a better future. If you can provide a vehicle that can give greater meaning and purpose to their efforts, amazing things are possible.

- **Much more leadership, not just more management.** To achieve any significant though routine task—as well as the uncountable number of repetitive tasks in an organization of even modest size—competent management from significant numbers of people is essential. Yes, you need leadership too, but the guts of the engine are managerial processes. Yet in order to capitalize on unpredictable windows of opportunity which might open and close quickly, and to somehow spot and avoid unpredictable threats, the name of the game is leadership, and not from one larger-than-life executive. The game is about vision, opportunity, agility, inspired action, passion, innovation, and celebration—not just project management, budget reviews, reporting relationships, compensation, and accountability to a plan. Both sets of actions are crucial, but the latter alone will not guarantee success in a turbulent world.

- **An inseparable partnership between the hierarchy and the network, not just an enhanced hierarchy.** The two systems, network and hierarchy, work as one, with a constant flow of information and activity between them—an approach that succeeds in part because the people essentially volunteering to work in the network already have jobs within the hierarchy. The dual operating system cannot be, and does not have to be, two super-silos, staffed by two different groups of full-time people, like the old Xerox PARC (an amazing strategic innovation machine) and Xerox corporate itself (which pretty much ignored PARC, or at least could never execute on the fantastic commercial opportunities it uncovered). And, ultimately, the meshing of the two parts succeeds as does anything new that at first seems awkward, wrong, or threatening: through education, role modeling from the top of the hierarchy, demonstrated success, and finally sinking into the very DNA of the organization, so it comes to feel just like, well, "the way we do things here."

These principles point to something very different than the default way of operating within a hierarchy: to drive change through a limited number of appointed people who are given a business case for a particular set of goals and who project-manage the process of achieving the goals in the case. That default process can work just fine when the pace needed is not bullet-like, the potential pushback from people is not ferocious, and the clarity of what is needed is high (and innovation requirements are therefore low). But, increasingly, that is not the world in which we are living.

Based on these principles, the action on the network side of a dual system is different from that on the hierarchy side. Both are systematic. They are just very different. It's not a matter of one side being hard and metrically driven while the other is fluffy or soft. We know less today about network processes like "creating short-term wins" than we do about hierarchical processes like operational planning or creating relevant metrics. But, just as action within a well-run hierarchy is far from control-oriented people doing whatever comes into their heads, action within a well-run network is very different from enthusiastic volunteers doing whatever they want.

Because action within networks accelerates activity, especially strategically relevant activity, I call its basic processes the Accelerators.

THE EIGHT ACCELERATORS

The network's processes resemble activity you usually find in successful, entrepreneurial contexts. They are much like my eight steps for leading change, only this time with top management launching a dynamic that creates many more active change drivers, a network structure integrated with the hierarchy, and processes that, once started, never stop.

These are the eight Accelerators:

1. **Create a sense of urgency around a Big Opportunity.** The first Accelerator is all about creating and maintaining a strong sense of urgency, among as many people as possible, around a Big

Opportunity an organization is facing. Building a dual system starts here. This is, in many ways, the secret sauce which allows behavior to happen that many who have grown up in mature organizations would think impossible.

Urgency, in the sense used here, is not just about this week's problems but about the strategic threats and possibilities flying at you faster

The eight Accelerators

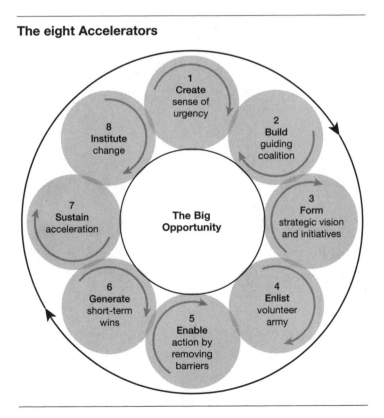

and faster. With Accelerator 1 working well, large groups of people, not just a few executives, rise each day thinking about how they might be able to help you pursue a Big Opportunity.

I have seen people devise dozens of creative ways to relentlessly build and maintain this sense of urgency. Doing this well is crucial, which is why I devote two chapters later in the book to growing urgency—especially through role modeling—and focusing it on a Big Opportunity.

2. **Build and evolve a guiding coalition.** The second Accelerator leverages off a greatly heightened and aligned sense of urgency to build the core of the network structure, then later to help it evolve into a stronger and more sophisticated form. This guiding coalition of people from across the organization deeply feels the urgency. These are individuals from all silos and levels who want to help you take on strategic challenges, deal with hyper-competitiveness, and win the Big Opportunity. They are people who want to lead, to be change agents, and to help others do the same. This core group has the drive, the intellectual and emotional commitment, the connections, the skills, and the information to be an effective

sun in your dynamic new solar system. These
are people who can, and do, learn how to work
together effectively as a large team.

With a sufficient sense of urgency, finding good people who want to participate in a
guiding coalition is surprisingly easy. Getting
individuals from different levels and silos to
work well together requires effort. Just throw
them into a room and they are likely to re-create
what they know: a management-centric hierarchy. But under the right conditions—with
urgency around a Big Opportunity as a crucial component—they will learn how to work
together in a totally new way. And with help,
both the guiding coalition and the organization's
executive committee will learn how to work
together in a way that allows for the hierarchy
side and the network side to stay strategically
aligned, to maintain high levels of reliability and
efficiency, and to develop a whole new capacity
for speed and agility.

3. **Form a change vision and strategic initiatives.**
    The third Accelerator has the guiding coalition
    clarify a vision that fits a big strategic opportu-
    nity and select strategic initiatives that can move
    you with speed and agility toward the vision.

When you first form a dual system, much of this, especially the initiatives, may already exist, created by the hierarchy's leadership team. But the initiatives the nascent network side attacks first will be those that individuals in the guiding coalition have great passion to work on. These will always be activities that the organization's executive committee agrees make great sense. But these will be initiatives which a management-driven hierarchy is ill equipped to handle well enough or fast enough by itself.

4. **Enlist a volunteer army.** In the fourth Accelerator, the guiding coalition, and others who wish to help, communicate information about the change vision and the strategic initiatives to the organization in ways that lead large numbers of people to buy into the whole flow of action. Done well, this process results in many individuals wanting to help, either with some specific initiative or just in general. This Accelerator starts to pull, as if by gravity, the planets and moons into the new network system.

5. **Enable action by removing barriers.** In the fifth Accelerator, everyone helping on the network side (the "right side" in the illustrations in this and the previous chapter) works swiftly

to achieve initiatives and find new ones that are strategically relevant. People talk, think, invent, and test, all in the spirit of an agile and swift entrepreneurial start-up. Much of the action here has to do with identifying and removing barriers which slow or stop strategically important activity. Within a dual system, and unlike in a start-up, this process guides people to pay close attention to their hierarchy: to what is being done there (to avoid overlap of effort), to what has been done there (to avoid plowing old ground), and to the hierarchy's operational goals and incremental strategic initiatives (to maintain alignment). Smart actions, based on good information from all silos and levels, are taken with heightened speed.

6. **Generate (and celebrate) short-term wins.** The sixth Accelerator is about everyone on the network side helping to create an ongoing flow of strategically relevant wins, both big and very small. Action here also ensures that the wins are as visible as possible to the entire organization and that they are celebrated, even if only in small ways. These wins, and their celebration, can carry great psychological power and play a crucial role in building and sustaining a dual

system. They give credibility to the new structure. This credibility in turn promotes more and more cooperation within the overall organization. These wins draw out respect, understanding, and eventually complete cooperation from the most control-oriented managers, who themselves have no desire to be network-side volunteers.

7. **Sustain acceleration.** Accelerator 7 keeps the entire system moving despite a general human tendency to let up after a win or two. It is built on the recognition that so many wins come from sub-initiatives which, by themselves, may be neither substantial nor particularly useful in a strategic sense. Larger initiatives will lose steam and support unless related sub-initiatives are also completed successfully. Here, with relentless energy focused forward on new opportunities and challenges, we find a motor which helps all the other Accelerators keep going, as needed, like spark plugs and cylinders in a car's engine. It is the opposite of a one-and-done approach and mindset.

8. **Institute change.** Accelerator 8 helps institutionalize wins, integrating them into the hierarchy's processes, systems, procedures, and behavior—

in effect, helping to infuse the changes into the culture of the organization. When this happens with more and more changes, there is a cumulative effect. After a few years, such action drives the whole dual operating system approach into an organization's very DNA.

When these Accelerators are all functioning well, they naturally solve the challenges inherent in building a new and different kind of organization. They provide the energy, the volunteers, the coordination, the integration of hierarchy and network, and the needed cooperation. As they capitalize on opportunities and work around threats, the whole system grows and accelerates. Eventually it becomes the way you do business in a rapidly changing world. You move ahead of tough competition or achieve fiercely ambitious goals. And, done right, all this happens without adding expensive staff, disrupting daily operations, or missing earnings targets.

THE VOLUNTEER ARMY

The people who drive these processes and populate the Accelerator network also help make the daily business of the organization hum. They're not a separate group of consultants, new hires, or task force appointees.

We have found that just 5 to 10% of the managerial and employee population in a hierarchy is all you need to make the network function beautifully. This point is central to making the whole dual system work, for two reasons. First, because they work in the hierarchy, these 5 to 10% have crucial organizational knowledge, relationships, credibility, and influence. They are often the first to see threats or opportunities—and they have the zeal to deal with them if put into a structure where that is possible. Second, they add no new (perhaps impossibly large) budget item.

With Accelerator 1 working well, and the resulting sense of urgency high enough, it is actually easy to find this volunteer army of individuals who bring energy, commitment, and genuine enthusiasm. Modest but aligned actions, taken by many passionate people who bring with them insight from all levels and all silos, imbue the network with the power it needs to undertake smart, strategic action.

People who have never seen this sort of dual operating system work often worry, quite logically, that a bunch of enthusiastic volunteers might create more problems than they solve—by running off and making ill-conceived decisions and disrupting daily operations. Here is where the network structure, the underlying principles, and the accelerating processes all come into play. They create conditions under which people generate not just ideas, but ideas backed by good data from all silos and levels in a hierarchy. They create conditions under which people do not just develop initiatives, but understand that it is their job to implement them. They create conditions which guide people not just to keep daily operations running smoothly, but to improve day-to-day processes to make the work of the organization easier, more efficient, less costly, and more effective.

In organizations where a dual system has really taken hold, individuals have told me that the rewards from working in the network can be tremendous—though they are rarely monetary. They talk about the fulfillment they get from pursuing a broader, enterprise-wide mission they believe in. They appreciate the chance to collaborate with a broader array of people than they ever could have worked with in their regular jobs within the hierarchy. A number of them say that their strategy work has led to increased visibility across the organization and to better positions in the hierarchy. And their managers often come to appreciate how the volunteers develop professionally. Consider this e-mail I received from a client in Europe: "I can't believe how quickly this second operating system gives growth to real talents within the organization. Once people feel 'Yes, I can do it!' they also start faster growth in their regular jobs in the hierarchy, which helps make today's operations more effective."

The dual operating system: Key characteristics

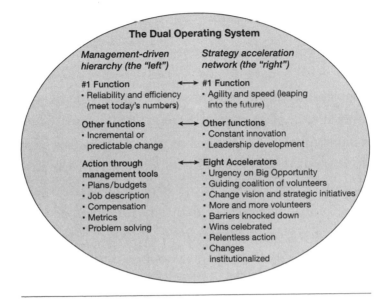

The Dual Operating System

Management-driven hierarchy (the "left")		Strategy acceleration network (the "right")
#1 Function • Reliability and efficiency (meet today's numbers)	←→	**#1 Function** • Agility and speed (leaping into the future)
Other functions • Incremental or predictable change	←→	**Other functions** • Constant innovation • Leadership development
Action through management tools • Plans/budgets • Job description • Compensation • Metrics • Problem solving	←→	**Eight Accelerators** • Urgency on Big Opportunity • Guiding coalition of volunteers • Change vision and strategic initiatives • More and more volunteers • Barriers knocked down • Wins celebrated • Relentless action • Changes institutionalized

GROWING AND BUILDING
MOMENTUM ORGANICALLY

A dual operating system doesn't start fully formed and doesn't require a sweeping overhaul of the organization—hence there is much less risk than one might think. It evolves, growing organically over time, accelerating action to deal with a hyper-competitive world, and taking on a life that seems to differ in the details from company to company. It can start with small steps. Version 1.0 of a right-side, strategy-accelerator network may arise in only one part of an enterprise—say, the supply chain system or the European group. After it becomes a powerful force there, it can expand into other parts of the organization.

Version 1.0 may also play no role in strategy formulation or adjustment, but concentrate only on agile and innovative implementation. It may feel at first more like a big employee-engagement exercise that, indeed, produces a much bigger payoff without increasing the payroll. But the network and the Accelerators evolve, and momentum comes faster than you might expect. As long as the executive committee understands the new system and plays its role, and as long as the new organization does indeed help with competitive challenges, the whole dual system model will eventually seep into the culture as "the way we do things here."

Not surprisingly, there are challenges. Over the past seven years, my team has aided any number of pioneers—in the private and public sectors, functional departments, product divisions, or at corporate—in building dual operating systems. The challenges are fairly predictable, and not insignificant. One is ensuring that the two parts of the system learn to work together well. Here it is essential that the core of the network (the guiding coalition) and the executive committee learn to develop and maintain the right relationship. Another is building momentum: the most important step here is to create and communicate wins from the very start.

Probably the biggest challenge is how to make people who are accustomed to control-oriented hierarchies believe that a dual system is even possible. Education can help. The right attitude from the top of the hierarchy helps greatly. But again, this is why a rational and compelling sense of urgency around a big strategic opportunity is so important. Once it has been sparked, mobilizing the guiding coalition and putting the remaining Accelerators in motion can happen almost organically. It doesn't jolt an enterprise the way sudden dramatic organizational change does. It doesn't require you to build something gigantic and then flick a switch to get it going (while praying that it works). And in a world where capital is constrained in so many organizations, the incremental cost of this approach is, incredibly, almost nothing. Think of it as a vast, inexpensive, purposeful, and structured expansion—in scale, scope, and power—of the smaller, informal networks that accomplish important tasks faster and cheaper than hierarchies can.

The inevitable failures of single operating systems hurt us now. I believe they are going to kill us in the future. The twenty-first century will force us all to evolve toward a fundamentally new form of organization. The good news is that this can allow us to do much more than simply hang onto what we have achieved in the twentieth century. If we successfully implement a new way of running organizations, we can take advantage of the strategic challenges in a rapidly changing world. We can actually make better products and services, enlarge wealth, and create more and better jobs, all more quickly than we have done in the past. That is, while the consequences of an increasingly changing world do have a downside, they also have a potentially huge upside.

We still have much to learn. Nevertheless, the companies that get there first, because they are willing to pioneer action now, will see immediate and long-term success—for shareholders, customers, employees, and themselves. I am convinced that those who lag will suffer greatly—if they survive at all.

THREE

THE STAKES
A Cautionary Tale

The following case, like all stories, is idiosyncratic in its details. But the fundamental challenges this firm faced are becoming the norm today.

As you read, keep this question in mind: does any of this seem familiar?

A NEW STRATEGY

The firm offers professional services. It was third in market share in its industry. Intensified global competition along with rapid advances in technology could have pushed it into fourth place, which is not a good place to be. The CEO retired and the board brought in someone from the outside who was seen as a visionary and had developed a superb reputation in a smaller firm in a closely related sector. Once on the job, the new

CEO immediately set up a study group, which he led. He pulled some managers off their jobs to be in the group full time and hired a well-known consulting firm to help. The mandate: calculate what will likely happen with no changes in strategic direction and determine what the biggest opportunities were for gaining new strategic advantage. The CEO clearly had opinions on both points, which he was not bashful in sharing with the group, but he insisted on aggressive gathering of facts and rigorous analysis.

Four months later the executive committee is presented with a report from the group which demonstrates that current policies could easily lead to a slide into fourth place in their industry, and that the economic consequences from such a slide would be serious. The report also highlights a number of very lucrative strategic opportunities. The CEO likes the most aspirational of these, which would have the firm deliver a significantly different product to its customers, one which customers say would be a "dream" solution to one of their most pressing needs. In essence, it would be a version of what the firm has already been selling, but in a form that would be simpler and easier for customers to use. Some new start-ups in its industry have shown such a course to be possible, but they do not have the visibility, scale, financial strength, or field organization to pose much of a threat to the established players—yet.

The new CEO argues that if they move quickly, they could execute this strategy before their larger competitors even seriously consider it, not least because the big competitors are older, more bureaucratic, and slower. Relying on the impressive data that has been gathered and analyzed by the study group and consultants, the CEO demonstrates that, if successful, the new strategy could catapult the firm into first place in five years, enable it to hold on to that position, and add $1 billion to its market capitalization. After much discussion, the executive committee buys the case, and after even further discussion, so does the board.

The business case calls for an aggressive acquisition program, starting in about one year, to gobble up all of the new start-ups which are already pursuing the dream strategy, and one smaller but established player that seems to be moving in that direction. The case also calls for several other supplementary initiatives to be executed as quickly as possible. One of these is to put in place a global human resources information technology system, which would give management accurate, real-time information on personnel costs, fully loaded (i.e., not just salaries for all employees worldwide, but also benefits, company cars, office leases for all new facilities for added employees, and so forth). Since this is a professional services firm, these costs add up to a very high percentage of total expenses, and the current HR

IT systems are not able to provide real-time information on total employment, much less the total costs. The problem is becoming worse as the firm's global business grows and different areas rely on different, unintegrated systems.

THE HR IT INITIATIVE

An internal task force is set up. It puts out RFPs to systems consultants. They study the proposals and choose one. This process takes two months, which the IT people see as warp speed. The consultants, with guidance from the task force, fan out across the world and come back with a recommendation for a single global system. It is more complex than the firm needs now, but the consultants argue persuasively that a simpler system will have to be replaced within a few years, and the total costs of two implementations will be considerably more than "doing it right" the first time. The task force finally agrees and runs the plan by the executive committee. The CEO does not love the complexity, the timing, or the cost. But the IT consultants are the best in the business, so the plan is approved with the caveat "Do it fast, keep on budget, and minimize any disruptions to current business operations."

A more detailed plan is developed. It is given to a program management office, and a senior project manager is selected. The consultants and the task force stay involved to help do the work. And off they go.

ASSESSING THE STAKES

A programming supervisor in the Miami office is asked about the stakes involved in getting the new global HR IT initiative done right—on time, on budget, functioning well, and not creating problems for others. He says:

"I have a budget of $25,000 for some additional help. I think this is realistic, but I've never done anything like this on a global basis."

"What about the stakes for the company of this project going very well versus poorly?"

"The entire company?"

"Yes."

"I have no idea. That's above my pay grade."

"Guess."

"It certainly is talked about a lot. So it's not just another project."

"So the stakes of this to the company . . .?"

"I really don't know. My best guess, and it is a guess, would be six figures. Maybe even high six figures."

Ask his boss the same question and he says:

> "This project has a global budget, I think, of around $8 million."

> "So the stakes . . .?"

> "Define 'stakes.'"

> "However you think of it."

> "I suppose we could waste a few million. Or more. But that's very unlikely."

Ask the same question of the corporate head of HR and he says:

> "About a half million dollars is our own budget for this. Almost all the rest is in IT."

> "Stakes for the company?"

> "It depends. The total budget for the global IT project you are talking about is $8 million. I hear it is trickier than it might seem for lots of reasons. You should be asking Sid [the head of IT], not me, about the chances of it going over budget or being late."

You do just that.

> "Stakes to the company?" asks Sid.

> "Yes."

"If we're late, the system won't be ready for the big acquisition program, the first phase of the service simplifications, and the like. The odds are that that won't matter much, but there is some small chance that we can't get costs clear enough fast enough and it could create hard-to-foresee difficulties."

"So the stakes for the company?"

"More than is obvious for a project with a budget of $8 million. Certainly in the millions, possibly even beyond the eight, which is why we are giving it serious attention."

You ask the CFO.

"George [the CEO] has a bold vision of what we can do over the next five years. To move ahead, we have something like ten or eleven big projects to put us firmly into a position to pursue the opportunity. The last time I looked, the total cost of the initiatives was $107 million. For us, that is a huge number. So—no small stakes. The IT project for HR systems is a small piece of that, but, you could argue, certainly not an unimportant piece. Problems with any of the projects could chip away at his goal of a $1 billion market cap bump. How much are the stakes for this specific project you are interested in? It's hard to say with any precision because we haven't done anything quite like this before. I'd certainly say in the tens of millions because of how it interacts with the acquisition strategy. Could be more. So, a larger figure than probably the IT people see."

Finally, you ask the CEO.

"I think the stakes of all these projects are bigger than would seem obvious because of how they interrelate to what we are going to do starting in eight months. If we get this right, and I am confident we will, the firm will be in a totally different place in five years, with a totally different set of prospects for the future. We're talking about a great deal of growth and potentially billions added to the value of the firm. But I've been through a similar drill once before at [his last, smaller, employer] and even though my team here doesn't have that sort of experience, I am confident we can pull this off."

You ask: "In terms of the HR IT project, what are the stakes for the firm of getting it done right?"

"It's hard to isolate any of the specific initiatives. What impact could it have if it came in, say, six months late and 50% over budget? Millions, obviously. If they really messed it up, which, since I will be watching it, is hard to conceive, it could cost us tens of millions. It's hard to believe a relatively simple $8–10 million project could somehow cost you $50 million over five years, but I suppose that is possible."

THE STORY, PART 2

The implementation of the HR IT initiative seems to go well for a while. Then the CEO's most important division manager is told by his technical people that the project will delay another initiative the sales organization is driving. This leads to meetings; new revenue forecasts from sales, which the CEO does not like; and strains among some of the sales, IT, and HR staffs.

Then the managers for four countries—including the most important one for the future, China—complain (quietly at first) that their people can't handle all the change initiatives and that this project in particular is a distraction because it is not well aligned with a major marketing initiative. The head of Eastern Europe says his IT people believe the choice of the specific HR system was a mistake made by American consultants and decision makers at corporate headquarters who don't understand his unique problems. The IT consultants say that the Eastern European management's ingrained habits and culture, built up over decades, make them very difficult to deal with.

Relations between corporate and the field grow testier, with excuses about delays and demands for more funding. The arguments flow over into interactions about other sales, client, and budgetary issues.

The consultants hired to help lead the new system implementation then announce that the HR systems in Latin America actually work very well, much better than the consultants had initially thought. But the systems are totally incompatible with the new software chosen, and the Latin American HR system is tightly linked to all the other IT systems in the area (for sales, manufacturing, and so on).

Hearing of this, the exasperated CEO asks why the problem was not identified earlier. The consultants say it's simply that they were asked to do a four-month project in two months. No other understandable answer is supplied, but a good guess is that the Latin American management team wasn't entirely forthcoming initially. They seem to have assumed that when more information about their systems was uncovered, they would be left alone to focus on tough revenue and income goals and all the other change initiatives. And it eventually does become very clear that the Latin American IT and HR staff think they should waste zero time on this initiative, since their systems are better than any in the company.

The head of the HR IT task force is replaced. This makes some people happy and others fearful. The new man brings in his own program manager, who starts setting new goals and timelines. A change management team is assembled. A senior executive (the head of HR) is formally designated the executive sponsor of the initiative.

Timelines slip, but people work exceptionally hard and the work does move along. But at the eight-month mark the new system is not fully up and tested. It's close, but there are significant kinks.

And then it happens.

The acquisition programs are launched. Without real-time information on the full cost picture, decisions are made during the normal end-of-quarter scramble that inadvertently increase expenses relative to revenues so that the firm misses earnings expectations. The financial markets, already wary of the company's aggressive moves, get spooked. The stock price drops 15% in one day. The CEO is apoplectic. His first major acquisition deal, almost closed, stalls. The biggest player in the industry swoops in and outbids what the CEO's board is willing to pay for the acquisition. This drives the firm's stock down even more, makes the additional acquisitions in process much more difficult, and gives the bigger competitor time to recover. That firm then begins following its own version of the CEO's strategy and starts to position itself to capitalize on his Big Opportunity. And over the next few years, it does.

The firm, which had had the very real possibility of rising from third place to first in its industry, slides to fourth. Market share and market capitalization go down slightly and do not entirely recover over the next five years. The difference in market cap between what happened and what could have happened is estimated by one respected industry analyst to be $1.5 billion or more. And this figure does not take into account the economics of the possible difference in strategic strength at year five to deal with the next five years. That additional figure, the analyst argues, could be in the range of $0.25–3 billion, bringing the total consequences of the failed HR IT project to between $1.75 billion and $4.5 billion.

The CEO's credibility within the firm crashes. A few key personnel leave. The basic story is reviewed many times in the press. But as for the underlying account of how one single piece of a big strategic change effort essentially killed wonderful possibilities and led to a host of unforeseen problems—that story never makes it into the news with any clarity.

REALITY VERSUS BELIEFS

Insiders estimated the stakes involved for properly executing the HR IT initiative were in the range of

$750,000 (from the Miami office programming supervisor) to $50 million (from the CEO). That means the assessment from most people in the firm was probably about .02% of reality. The most accurate guess, from only one person, the CEO, was about 1 or 2% of reality.

And none of this takes into account collateral damage: jobs not added because of lost opportunity (and remember that for every lost job, economists say that there are significant ripple effects that affect many dozens of people in large and small ways); the costs to customers in decreased quality of services due to disruptions (and in this case one big customer had in fact built its strategies on assumptions based on our firm's ambitious plans); intangible costs to the organization (when trust, collaboration, and morale take a hit and are not easily repaired). There is also the damage to individual reputations, careers, and legacies, which, for the CEO in this case, was very unpleasant.

Yet it could have been worse. Bankruptcy, or acquisition by another firm that then effectively destroys you—those are the real downside cases. And in a more turbulent and competitively fierce world, the downside is increasing for most enterprises. The number of organizations living on the equivalent of melting icebergs has never been greater.

However, the upside for enterprises has also never been greater. The kind of success that Google and

Facebook have achieved within five to ten years has never existed before. Never. And though the upside for the firm in this case wasn't at that level, it was considerable, with substantial benefits for employees, customers, owners, executive careers, tax revenues, and more still.

Some may read this story and say that a significant factor was simply bad luck. But our decisions and actions always increase the probability of what we call "luck," good or bad. And this firm made serious mistakes, starting with severely underestimating the stakes involved in its initiatives. Then, in trying to capitalize on a Big Opportunity, those involved used what they knew—tools which for the most part would be considered as "best practices" by nearly all enterprises today. These are practices based on and formed within a management-driven hierarchy—enhanced with strategy study groups, business cases, IT consultants, task forces, program management offices, executive sponsors of initiatives, and more—to execute new strategic initiatives. Collectively they constitute a vehicle that can move at sixty miles an hour with pretty good steering. Unfortunately, we are driving this system in a race with unpredictable turns and obstacles—one that can demand speeds of a hundred miles an hour with much more agile steering.

And that is the rub. With speed low enough and predictability high enough, certain methods work just fine in organizations. But these methods cannot possibly work when speed goes up significantly and predictability (predictably) goes down. It becomes a different game. You must be able to operate with more of the pace and agility you would see in a successful entrepreneurial firm or start-up. The business in this case did not have it—and did not even realize it did not have it. And this is the norm today.

You could argue, I suppose, that our CEO should not have pursued a bold new strategy. The company certainly was not in any short-term crisis. But the industry analysts today say, in retrospect, that the strategic study group was probably right in predicting that a stay-the-course approach would have dropped the firm to fourth place in its industry. Its market capitalization would undoubtedly have dropped. Its competitive vulnerability would have increased.

I know the individuals involved in this story, and you cannot make a case that they used the wrong methods because they weren't competent. The CEO is smart and was highly respected in his industry. Nevertheless, he and his people used a methodology for strategy execution that they automatically assumed would work. They never even stopped for a moment to think that they might be stuck in an outmoded system: a twentieth-century, single-system hierarchy that—no matter how heavily enhanced with strategy study groups, task forces, program managers, and consultants—put them at great risk from day one.

FOUR

LEADERSHIP AND EVOLUTION

We are in the midst of a storm that has been increasing in intensity for decades, driven by advancing technologies and global integration. Some sectors or industries are being hit more obviously and directly than others with turbulence, new competitive threats, technological discontinuities, new risks . . . and new opportunities. But no company is immune. Centuries-old DuPont, for one, was once able to compete with products having life cycles of close to twenty years; today, some of its products require the speed of two-year cycles. The newspaper industry, which operated with one business model for over a century, has blown up before our eyes in the past decade. PCs have always been a very competitive product, but if you are trying to run HP or Dell right now, "competitive" would sound like far too weak a word for the world in which you live.

Leading firms have been looking for and deploying new ways to deal with these new realities. In some cases, these practices have worked very well—up to now. But everything I have seen and all the evidence I can find suggests that today's "best practices" are producing less and less satisfying results.

Why is this? And why, logically, will this problem only grow bigger?

To convincingly answer these questions, one needs to confront two interrelated issues around which there is massive confusion. The first is the nature of management and the nature of leadership. Our misunderstanding of this issue makes us believe that a management-driven hierarchy with competent executives at the top ought to be able to guide an organization to move faster, be more agile, and thrive. It can't anymore.

The second issue surrounds the way enterprises naturally evolve over time. We tend to think that organizations go from very small hierarchies with few and relatively unsophisticated managerial processes to very large hierarchies with much more formal and sophisticated processes. And that is simply not so. Over time, successful organizations evolve from networks to hierarchies, and along the way quickly pass through a stage that looks very much like a dual system.

MANAGEMENT IS NOT LEADERSHIP

Listen to how most people talk in everyday conversation, and you'll find that they often use the words "management" and "leadership" interchangeably. If they do make a distinction in meaning, it is usually in reference to levels in a hierarchy. People at the very top provide "leadership"—whatever that is—or at least they are supposed to. People in the middle do the "management," again with little clarity about what that means. This way of thinking is inaccurate and increasingly troublesome.

Management is a set of well-known processes that help organizations produce reliable, efficient, and predictable results. Really good management helps us do well what we more or less know how to do regardless of the size, complexity, or geographic reach of an enterprise. These processes include planning, budgeting, structuring jobs, staffing jobs, giving people time-tested policies and procedures to guide their actions, measuring their results, and problem solving when results do not fit the plan.

Management as we know it today is almost entirely a later-twentieth-century invention. Although it has roots that go back centuries (as in running the Roman Empire), what we see today is a very modern phenomenon. Management now requires great skill. And both what it is and what it can achieve would have been difficult for even a well-educated person in the year 1900 to fully grasp.

Our sophisticated modern-day management processes did not exist in or prior to the nineteenth century because they simply weren't needed. After the Civil War in the United States, for example, there were only a few hundred organizations with over a hundred employees. Today the number of US organizations with over a hundred employees is well over a hundred thousand. In the year 1900, the number of firms that did business around the world, on all continents, was very close to zero. Today the number is so large it is hard to calculate.

Without competent management, the organizations that we have created in the last century, and that we continue to create today, could not function. Without management, chaos would reign. Enterprises would fall apart and go out of business quickly. Management is an incredibly important invention, yet the average person—even the average manager—has no real appreciation of what a marvel it is.

But management is not leadership.

Leadership is about setting a direction. It's about creating a vision, empowering and inspiring people to want to achieve the vision, and enabling them to do so with energy and speed through an effective strategy. In its most basic sense, leadership is about mobilizing a group of people to jump into a better future.

In many people's minds, great leadership tends to be associated with grand, larger-than-life figures—Abraham Lincoln, Queen Victoria—who mobilize their countrymen to take on some great cause and succeed beyond imagination. It is easy to think that such imposing and rare figures shape history through the power of their leadership, and only their leadership. But that was never the whole story, and we know for sure that this is most certainly not the way life works now.

Today you can find all sorts of people in all sorts of situations helping to provide at least some degree of leadership. A project engineer might take some initiative. Because of his or her leadership, a small group of people is mobilized to find and execute something new, creating results which others in the organization would have thought nearly impossible. You can find leadership

---

Management versus leadership

Management	Leadership
• Planning	• Establishing direction
• Budgeting	• Aligning people
• Organizing	• Motivating people
• Staffing	• Inspiring
• Measuring	• Mobilizing people to achieve astonishing results
• Problem solving	• Propelling us into the future
• Doing what we know how to do exceptionally well	
• Constantly producing reliable, dependable results	

---

coming from people who are officially called middle managers. And, conversely, you can sometimes find very little leadership in the actions of those near the top of a hierarchy.

More than anything, both today and throughout history, leadership has been associated with change. It's not about mobilizing a group to act the same way they have always acted. It has to do with changing people and their organizations so they can leap into a different and better future, no matter the threats or barriers or shifting circumstances.

In businesses today, leadership is the central force mobilizing people to create something that did not previously exist. That is, leadership creates an enterprise in the first place. And leadership takes existing enterprises and finds new opportunities, makes changes to capitalize on those opportunities, and moves firms into a future where they can grow and prosper.

Without sufficient leadership in a rapidly changing world, organizations become static and eventually fail. And by sufficient leadership, in organizations of any size, I do not mean a grand CEO or executive committee. There is no way that a single figure or a small team at the top of the hierarchy can provide all the leadership that is needed. A superman or -woman—even one supervising an exceptional group of managers, who in turn supervise highly talented individual contributors—can no longer do the job.

So which is more important? Management or leadership? To begin to answer that question, we need to look again at what role each plays. Management ensures the stability and efficiency necessary to run today's enterprise reliably. Leadership creates needed change to take advantage of new opportunities, to avoid serious threats, and to create and execute new strategies. The point is that management and leadership are very different, and when organizations are of any size and exist in environments which are volatile, *both are essential* to helping them win.

This takes us to possibly the most fundamental problem that organizations of all sorts are now facing. Any successful organization older than ten years and with more than thirty employees tends to have many people attending to the managerial chores and doing so at least adequately. It has to do so unless it has no short-term performance demands placed on it. Otherwise it can die, and rather quickly. But in most cases—especially when we are talking about more mature and larger organizations—sufficient leadership just isn't there. There is a substantial volume of research that draws this conclusion, and there is no credible research that I know of that supports the opposite conclusion.

The management/leadership matrix

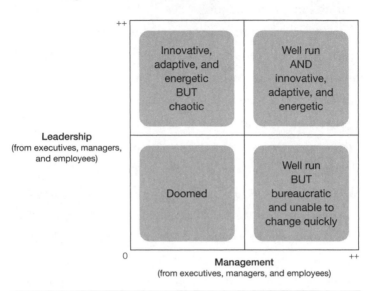

As long as the world is not changing much, the competition is not too fierce, and the strategic challenges are limited, you can survive with this reality. Performance measures may look very good. But: A world that is not very turbulent? A context in which competition for customers or budgets is not very fierce? This world is fast disappearing on us.

How did we get here? Why do we have this leadership problem? Here again there is much misunderstanding. And the best answer to these questions, I believe, is never discussed.

THE LIFE CYCLE OF ORGANIZATIONS

Highly successful start-ups have a rational, market-focused vision. Nearly everyone in these firms understands that vision, is committed to and aligned with it, and is inspired to work very hard. That is, there is some strong and effective leadership. It does not matter if the entrepreneur behind a venture is hoping to build a business around a new type of chocolate cookie sold to the public or a new type of microchip sold to other businesses. Leadership in a successful start-up can come largely from just a single entrepreneur, but typically others will play significant roles as well, with little acts of leadership helping the firm move forward.

In the early days, it's hard to find much management. There is rarely an organization chart in entrepreneurial success stories. Very often people will even smile at you if you ask for such a chart. There is good reason for this. Such enterprises have little traditional hierarchical management structure. If you were to diagram how they operate, the structure would look more like an ever-changing solar system or molecule. It's a network. It has a center, a sun, and various planets, some of which may have moons or even satellites of their own. The key entrepreneur is always the sun. Often he or she has one or two or three other key people also at the center.

The planets are not traditional functional areas—there isn't a marketing planet, a finance planet, an operations planet, and so on. The firm hasn't needed to think in those terms yet. Instead, the planets represent different kinds of initiatives, often associated with designing or testing new products and services.

Under these circumstances, it's hard to find much of a status hierarchy at all. A more junior person in the organization may look more important than the key entrepreneur. There are no offices of varying sizes associated with different levels of responsibility, as in a hierarchy. There are no strategic planning meetings or other standardized processes. Unless the enterprise is forced to put together a business plan in order to raise money, you won't find a hundred-page planning document anywhere.

All of these characteristics—the vision, the energy, the flat network, the ease of communication because there are no silos or levels or policies—can make this structure incredibly fast and agile. An initiative can be dropped in a day and a better idea can be pursued immediately. There is no need to have sixteen meetings, to fight people whose whole careers and salaries are tied to some initiative. This kind of agility can enable a successful young firm to run circles around more mature competitors.

With success in the market, such a young and effective enterprise grows. Then, at a certain point, it is forced to start building something that would look more familiar to us—even if the entrepreneur does not much like this change. Management structures and processes in their most elementary form start to be added because they are absolutely needed. A hierarchy starts to emerge, although at first it is very flat and usually does not even have clear job descriptions.

But in successful organizations, even as the managerial structure and processes begin to grow, the original entrepreneurial system does not go away. The energy around initiatives, the leadership from empowered people, the flexibility of working across groups—they all remain intact. The two systems coexist in a dual operating arrangement that is totally organic. Often what holds the two parts together and minimizes any conflict is the entrepreneur, who becomes a CEO and remains as the center of the start-up network. As a matter of natural evolution, and also out of economic necessity, people are not allowed to dedicate themselves full time to their original network activities and to have no place in the hierarchy. Thus strong human connections between the hierarchy and the network tie the two systems together.

It has been my observation that this period in a successful organization's life cycle is really quite extraordinary.

You see very profitable growth and, often, a unique and wonderful culture. Capital markets notice, too—and this only makes such organizations more successful.

If a firm continues to prosper, its operational needs correspondingly increase and the management-driven hierarchy grows and grows. More processes are added. For a while, the network itself might also grow, as more and more hires play a role in the various initiatives that are seeking opportunities and helping the organization remain agile.

But at some point in the company's continuing success, the hierarchy grows so large that it begins to dwarf the network. Sometimes a group of the original employees leave because they do not like what they perceive to be a "bureaucracy." All of this leads to growing tensions between the agile, fast, opportunity-seeking network and the reliable, efficient, stability-creating hierarchy. Since the hierarchy side of the organization tends to control resources, and because at a certain point it becomes much larger than the network side, it begins to quietly yet systematically kill off the network side of an organization. This is not a malicious act. It just happens, naturally.

The hierarchy grows, the network shrinks, and at a certain point what remains is essentially the look and feel and operation of a typical modern organization. It is not a matter of ending up with 100% management and 0% leadership. The mature, management-driven hierarchy will always have some leadership, almost always at the very top. But the look (structure) and the engine (processes) are essentially just the left side—the hierarchy side of the dual-system illustrations in chapters 1 and 2.

In the case in which the network side doesn't entirely disappear, you can sometimes find fragmented pieces of it operating underneath the hierarchy's radar. Or there might be invisible, informal organizations buried in corners of the hierarchy, no longer coordinated as a system. Some of the former knowledge or practices may remain, built around, say, one of the original project engineers now working in the production department. But the entrepreneurial network is gone—and with it the aligned vision, passion, agility, and speed.

Over time, this flow, represented in the accompanying diagram, seems to be an almost universal pattern in the life cycle of organizations. Sometimes the flow is smooth and gradual. In other cases it can happen rapidly or in fits and starts. There are inevitable bumps along the way as people are forced to adapt to new ways of operating. Ingrained habits, fear of the new and untested, and a natural suspicion of hierarchy among entrepreneurial types all add to the challenge.

At the end of this journey, a successful organization may have established a strong market position, powerful economies of scale, a robust brand presence, and good relations with customers. But in the drive for growth and success, something important was lost. While the firm is surviving well, and making good money, it does not have the innovative edge, or speed, or agility it once had. Its growth slows—and then slows further. Sometimes more nimble competitors will take away enough customers that pressure on prices begins to shrink margins. But it has enough presence, size, and financial strength

Typical life cycle of an organization: Network to hierarchy

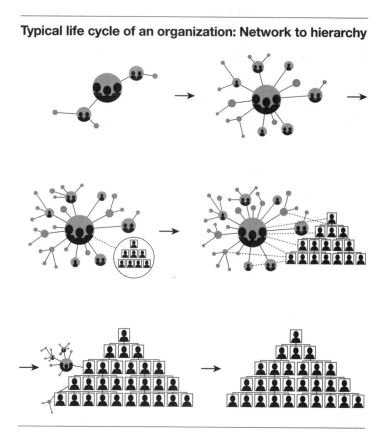

to continue operating in this way for some time, and it most certainly does not collapse and disappear. It is even possible, by following a number of "best practices," for mature, slow-moving, management-driven hierarchies to grow. We have seen most organizations rely on some of these practices in the last few decades. But increasingly they represent at best a delaying tactic.

These best practices come in three forms. Leaders have used them—and still use them today—to great effect in relatively still waters. In the first of the three, you simply stretch the time horizon for planning and the execution of plans. So, on a yearly basis, you do not only operational planning (looking out one year) but also "strategic planning" (looking out beyond a year). Then you execute in the normal way but with a longer time horizon built into plans and budgets. In the second case, you augment your hierarchy and management processes with new departments (for "strategic planning," "change management," and the like), new people (often to staff those departments), temporary task forces (or "tiger teams," "workstreams," and so on), and new relationships between boxes on the organizational chart (for example, task forces have executive "sponsors"). In the third practice, you try to buy, not build, new capability. You acquire enterprises which have already executed the strategy you desire or that have the agility and speed you need. The case in chapter 3 included bits of all three of these solutions. But the HR

IT initiative relied mostly, as is typically the case these days, on the second (augmentation).

The fundamental problem with all of these methods is that they build off a management-driven hierarchical system. They all build on a base created for stability, reliability, and efficiency. Yes, with good leadership you can use elongated planning and execution time frames, all sorts of new departments and task forces, as well as acquisitions to give you more speed and agility. But the base, the core of the system, defines its limits.

Such best practices are like ornaments—some delightful, to be sure—on a holiday tree. But no matter how pretty the decorations, it's still a holiday tree (in this case a management-driven hierarchy designed for efficiency and reliability). After a while, if you keep adding lights and streamers and amazing stars on top, the tree will start to look less, not more, appealing. If you still continue to decorate, at some point the tree will fall over. And from all I have seen, any enterprise, even the likes of Facebook or Google, is vulnerable to this very natural organizational evolution.

BACK TO THE FUTURE

What should be done? Some people think that we should simply declare mature organizations as hopeless and shut them down, to be replaced by new and vibrant enterprises. But we know of no way to deal with tens of millions of people regularly being thrown out of work and onto the job market. And large, mature organizations can be remarkably efficient, allowing them to offer goods at low prices, and be remarkably reliable, allowing those same goods to be produced with consistent quality.

For mature organizations, the needed path today is not to shut them down or crush them. The way forward is almost "back to the future"—but not all the way back to the time when firms were new and very small. The needed path leads to a new version of a stage that all successful organizations pass through. It is a stage in which they employ a dual operating system—that produces agility, speed, reliability, *and* efficiency. It is ideal for the rapid-fire world into which we are moving. And we know that creating such systems is possible. Thousands and thousands of organizations have done so in their evolution over time.

Dual systems are a natural part of the evolutionary journey of all successful firms. We just haven't noticed this happening for many reasons. We haven't been looking for dual systems. Firms going through that stage have not been aware of how they themselves were operating. Most people in mature organizations were not there to see the dual-system stage as it occurs early in an organization's life cycle. And the dual systems that occur naturally do not naturally sustain themselves.

Nearly two decades ago a few enterprises took steps in a back-to-the-future direction. They usually were dealing with a single large-scale strategic change. A few achieved remarkable results. Among well-known firms, these would include General Electric—which increased its market capitalization from $19 billion to $350 billion, a feat no financial analyst would have ever predicted for a big old firm operating in mature industries—and IBM—which dodged a bullet going directly at its heart as it reinvented itself as a services instead of a products company. I have documented what dozens and dozens of much-lesser-known enterprises have done in numerous books, including *Leading Change, The Heart of Change, Our Iceberg Is Melting, A Sense of Urgency,* and *Buy-in.*

Today there are organizations—not many, but a few—that have taken further steps toward creating sustainable dual systems. What pioneers have done does not come naturally to organizations, at least now. It happens because people take self-conscious actions. Although the details seem to vary from situation to situation, a basic pattern does not. It is all based on a few principles. It is all driven by a few processes. It creates results that go from very good to astonishing in contexts in which the stakes have been growing and the downside possibilities are grave.

In the next chapter, I will show you one case of how that happened.

FIVE

THE FIVE PRINCIPLES AND EIGHT ACCELERATORS IN ACTION

Accelerating an organization, making it faster and more nimble in dealing with strategic challenges, is never easy. Knowing the difference between leadership and management is crucial. Understanding your firm's entrepreneurial origins will help. But building a fully working and sustainable dual system is not simply a matter of replicating the past or pushing your managers to lead more and manage less.

In chapter 2 I described briefly the principles and processes that define a dual system. The principles set the foundation. The Accelerator processes, guided by those principles, are the basic building blocks. They begin creating the system as soon as they engage your biggest strategic challenge or opportunity; then they continue to build and reinforce the system in an organic way, becoming stronger and more self-sustaining, giving you the agility and speed to deal with an ever faster-moving and more volatile world.

This method for helping organizations evolve to a new stage (which in fact resembles an earlier phase) can be launched regardless of your current position—whether you are an organization run by a basic management-driven hierarchy, one run by a hierarchy with planning and execution processes stretched to include longer time frames, an organization designed as a hierarchy augmented by all sorts of new staff and departments and reporting relationships, any of the previous states supplemented by certain types of acquisitions, or even an organization at an earlier state in its evolution, not already in the mature quadrant but proceeding relentlessly, predictably, on a path that will lead it to one of the states just listed.

To help you take the next step in understanding how this all works, I again, as in chapter 3, provide a case study. Every situation is unique, of course, but there is much here that seems to be typical.

THE CASE OF DAVIDSON'S FIELD ORGANIZATION

Paul Davidson, the top sales executive in one division of a B2B technology firm, had seen sales growth slip for over twenty-four months. Revenues continued to go up, but at a slower and slower pace. When he concluded that his division had to be losing market share, he commissioned an outside study to give him more information along with recommendations for action. The study arrived four months later, and the data indeed showed that market share was down by slightly less than 4 percentage points over the prior two years, leaving Davidson's firm in fifth place in an industry dominated by one competitor.

Part of the problem, the consultants reported, was that Davidson's organization had lagged behind two of its competitors in setting up operations in Asia. Part of the problem was that customers were buying more products indirectly, through intermediaries, and the leader in his industry had jumped on this trend faster than Davidson's organization. The consultants reported that no one firm had clearly superior products, but with shrinking life cycles Davidson was always vulnerable on the product side. The data also strongly suggested that his sales costs per unit sold were high, for a number of historical reasons, especially compared to the costs for the number 1 and 2 players in his industry. High costs meant lower margins. It also made Davidson's boss reluctant to fund ideas from some of his people, who had already seen the field problems developing.

The consultants argued that the measures needed to turn all this around were not marginal adjustments but significant changes. They also spelled out an implementation process not unlike what Davidson had successfully used in the past, with a project management organization at the center of the activity, a number of task forces, executive sponsors, regular reports to his executive team, and a governance structure on top of everything. But Davidson judged that the suggested methods would never produce the sort of change needed within the time frame required.

Armed with the strategy study (minus the section on implementation), he initiated discussions with his own direct reports, his division head, and the firm's CEO. The goal was to gain support for several dynamic initiatives and leeway to execute the initiatives as he saw fit. When the CEO finally agreed, and others did not push back, Davidson moved forward by first looking for a method that he believed would suit his needs.

He more or less stumbled upon a body of research that was identifying the whole dual-systems approach. In retrospect, he says, there was much about the Accelerators and the hierarchy-network structure that he did not understand at first. But the underlying principles, at least intuitively, made sense to him.

THE FIVE PRINCIPLES AS PRESENTED TO DAVIDSON

The principles were essentially described to Davidson this way.

Acceleration demands many, many more change agents, not just the few usual appointees. Davidson was told that a management-driven hierarchy, even with intelligent enhancements, brings a relatively small number of people into important roles in strategic acceleration activities, where people can initiate and not just follow orders. But to produce faster and much more agile action you must significantly increase this number. Not by 50%, but more like 500% or 1000%. That's the first principle: you need a radical increase in the number of people involved in creating or executing strategic initiatives. The usual approach—a few task forces, an executive sponsor or two, a project manager or two, all positions filled with appointees you too often rely upon—won't come close to cutting it.

Davidson was told he would never unleash many change agents without a "get-to" and "want-to" philosophy, instead of a "have-to" one. A traditional single system appoints people—hopefully the right people—who then have a new job to do, often in addition to their regular work. Even when a hierarchy appoints a larger number of people (which is rare), it doesn't create a significant number of energized change agents. It typically creates hordes of managers and employees who will reluctantly go to meetings, unless they can find a way out. Accelerator processes achieve remarkable results because they are based on a simple insight: when you find energized people producing effective change, you almost always find people who want to do just that and feel that they have been given permission to do so. You do not find busy, harassed people who feel they have been stuck with one more set of tasks. So, principle number 2: it's all about volunteers.

Davidson was told that both head and heart must pull people in, not just the former. The principle inherent in a traditional hierarchical system is the belief that logic (a good business case) and money are the essential ingredients in motivating people to accept their appointments as change agents. The proven principle in a network system is that people will want to be change agents, will volunteer, and will do extra work without extrinsic carrots if they feel the task is rational—but much more so because they feel some true passion for the work. With that passion, it is amazing what people will do—and at no additional cost.

Furthermore, much more leadership, Davidson was told, is both key and feasible. It is not a matter of much more management. A strategy-accelerator network cannot be chaos. Its affairs need to be managed. But the crucial mindsets and behaviors—those that initiate action without waiting for higher-ups to give orders, that imagine what could be done rather than just figuring out what needs to be done within normal bounds, that help people enthusiastically buy into decisions about what to do, that creatively overcome obstacles to achievement, and that relentlessly work until opportunities are capitalized on—these are all leadership behaviors. They don't have to be grand, Churchillian actions. They can be quite modest. But the effect is cumulative. Many, many of these acts add up to the force required to accelerate crucial action. So, principle number 4: leadership, leadership, leadership.

Finally, Davidson was told that although two systems are required for acceleration, they must act as one organization. This seems self-evident, but it is a crucial overarching principle. A strategy accelerator network, to be effective, must work seamlessly and organically with the management-driven hierarchy, so that the whole organization is both getting today's job done with efficiency and reliability, constantly and incrementally improving itself, and handling today's increasing strategic challenges with speed and agility.

Davidson was told that the Accelerators which build and then run the network side of an organization are all founded on these basic ideas. The Accelerators ensure that a dual system's achievements—and the network itself—are sustainable over time. The eight processes ensure that a very powerful system does not evaporate, as it would tend to do in the natural evolution of an organization's life cycle.

ACCELERATOR 1: URGENCY ALIGNED AROUND A BIG OPPORTUNITY

Davidson convened the sales division's ten-person executive committee for a day-long meeting. He told his team that it was becoming clearer in his own mind what was required: a broader range of intermediaries to buy and distribute his products as a part of their larger customer solutions; the ability to move into the marketplace with new products faster; more focus on high-growth Asian markets; and a less costly sales operation. These challenges, he said, offered them opportunities to have a significant impact on the whole division, not just the field organization. But he felt strongly that they had to move quickly. He also told them that the consultants had clearly demonstrated that expenses were already high; thus hiring new people to accelerate any strategic moves was an unrealistic approach. So they needed to get much more out of their current people. Simply pushing harder was not going to be the solution, as many of their people were already working long hours.

Their challenge for the day, he said, was to jump-start a process of creating a heightened sense of urgency, among as many of their people as possible, about their strategic needs and possibilities.

Davidson asked his team to spell out their Big Opportunity and its impact—a statement or goal to which everyone in the room that day could commit. He wanted it to be positive, short, clear, and energizing—no gloom and doom or threatening consequences. He also wanted a message that even the most analytical of their people would have difficulty shooting down. Most importantly, it needed to be something that would mobilize as many of their people as possible—make them want to get up in the morning to contribute to needed strategic changes. Not sit on the sidelines. Not fight change. Not go off in ten different directions. And the starting place, Davidson said, was for his team to create a message they deeply believed was right and that inspired *them*. He was clear on this: the point was not to develop some "motivating communication" that would in turn be handed to his communications department to cascade down the hierarchy.

They began by talking about customer buying trends, shifting technology, and what competitors seemed to be doing. By 4:00 p.m., with some skilled facilitation, small- and large-group exercises, and a relentlessly positive tone, they succeeded in developing a very simple four-point statement along these lines:

- *We are convinced we have an opportunity to increase our sales growth significantly in two years, and to become the best sales organization in the industry.*

- *This is realistic because (1) customer needs are changing, requiring competitors to change, but it is*

*not certain they can change fast enough; (2) markets
in developing countries are starting to grow explo-
sively; and (3) we are clearly not operating at peak
efficiency within the company.*

- *We have not changed fast enough to keep up with
  external demands, even though we have excellent
  people. We are capable of changing faster—we've
  done it in the past when we were smaller.*

- *If we handle this right, there is no reason why we
  cannot create an exceptionally successful field organization of which everyone—starting with us—will
  be deeply proud to be a part.*

This may not sound so exciting. But by the end of the
meeting, about half of the team members were clearly,
visibly energized. Why? These were the individuals
who were not happy with the current situation and
seemed to very much want to work for a firm willing to
pursue an aggressive agenda. A few others were mostly
on board, because they understood that changes were
needed; they knew that whatever success they were
having in making such strategic shifts was coming too
slowly; and they believed if they could get more sales
people and sales managers aligned around a simple set
of ideas it might help greatly. The last two executives in
the room could not conceive of how this exercise would

be useful, and they worried that it actually had downside risks for them.

The Frankfurt-based head of the European group was in the first category. A star athlete while in college, he had never believed in aiming for anything less than a gold medal. The sales division's finance head was in the second category. His inclination was to solve the expense problems by simply cutting everyone's budgets substantially. But he was sophisticated enough to know that some groups (like Europe) might go into open rebellion, with all the uncertain consequences. And the opportunity statement made bold projections about the potential increase in revenues but included nothing about the need to increase head count or other expenses, giving him more leverage in budget talks to push the conversation in ways he deemed rational. One of the two skeptics was the person who headed the biggest region, and the one with the most problems. He was not happy for many reasons: his organization did not have the capacity to take on more work; he was a very control-oriented manager and didn't like the uncertainties inherent in this new initiative; he was afraid he might end up in a position where what was expected from his organization would not be deliverable; and, probably (if only unconsciously), he worried that he could be placed in a politically precarious position.

At the end of the meeting, one of Davidson's staff (from the first category) volunteered to organize a team to continue what had been started that day—creating a much-heightened sense of strategic urgency throughout the organization. Davidson was adamant that they not appoint one more task force, so the team eventually came to be made up of twenty-one volunteers from across the field globally. As a group, the twenty-one had broad credibility and came from multiple levels in the hierarchy. They wanted faster change and embraced—intellectually and emotionally—what came to be called their "Big Opportunity" statement. These people agreed on an ambitious goal: to get a minimum of half of the four-thousand-member sales organization to sincerely support the statement and start behaving accordingly.

This "urgency team" spent three months devising and implementing ideas for forging a broad understanding of, passion for, and commitment to the ideas in the Big Opportunity statement. They had a team teleconference once every two weeks, but the real work went on in ten subgroups, each of which worked slightly differently.

The teams organized meetings with salespeople, developed support materials for first-line sales managers to engage their groups, and built an intranet portal filled with information, videos, blogs, and stories about the ways in which individuals on the sales team were already changing. The urgency subgroups were creative. But most of all, they were relentless.

More opportunistically, they took advantage of the annual three-day sales management meeting scheduled for one month after their group had been formed. The meeting that year was focused on cloud computing, with planned attendance of about four hundred, and a program of internal and external speakers. An urgency subteam convinced the organizers to redesign nearly a quarter of the agenda to focus directly or indirectly on the urgency statement, strategic possibilities, and the need for change.

At the meeting, some of team's ideas were not exactly hits. The more cynical in the crowd had great fun with the "I'm in" pins that were handed out. But some ideas turned out to be very powerful. A twenty-minute, unrehearsed speech from one of the older and most respected urgency team members had real impact. He talked about why he had first joined the firm and how much he wanted to see happen—quickly—before he retired. The talk visibly moved many people in the audience.

There was one quick and unexpected result of this exercise: some people *immediately* started taking small, impromptu actions to push the field group toward the opportunity. When the results of these actions actually led to meaningful outcomes—no matter how small— they came to be called "wins," and the urgency team started to keep track of them and add them to their portal.

The urgency team's success started quickly; leveled off at the end of the quarter, when everyone was hustling to close business and meet sales targets; then ramped up exponentially as larger and larger groups of people in the organization talked—sometimes analytically, sometimes emotionally—to their colleagues about the Big Opportunity.

ACCELERATOR 2:
THE GUIDING COALITION

Just before the team decided they had hit their target, or come close, Davidson sent out an e-mail inviting employees to apply for a one-year role at the core of a new kind of organization he wanted to build. The application form asked why a person wanted to be on the guiding coalition, the "GC," how he or she planned to manage the additional workload, and what ideas the individual had for taking advantage of the Big Opportunity. It explained only in very general terms what the GC would do: attract and help guide other volunteers who would accelerate movement toward capitalizing on the four-point message in the Big Opportunity statement. Despite the vagueness of the assignment—and yet complete clarity that this role would be in addition to their regular jobs—210 people applied for thirty-five slots.

Skeptics were surprised that so many applied. But as one of Davidson's executive team members pointed out, the number was not irrationally high. After the urgency exercise, over two thousand people in the field organization had said they were in the game. Of them, 10% volunteered for the additional position. Since the urgency team had done such a good job, was 10% really such a shocking number?

A subteam of the urgency group made the initial pass at selecting the thirty-five. Most of the people chosen were from middle management and below. All of the company's geographic areas around the world had some representation. Two people who reported to Davidson were included, along with three executive or administrative assistants. All were selected because, among other criteria, they had written very compelling applications, were reputed to have credibility among the people with whom they normally interacted, and showed no signs of being overtly political in their motivation, hoping only to advance their careers or protect their turf. The sales executive committee signed off on the group, insisting on only one change: turning away a person they feared was already working 120% in a critically important "left-side" job. Davidson immediately sent a note to the thirty-five explaining that they had been selected and, in general terms, why. He thanked them for volunteering to help the organization accelerate on such an important journey.

He also sent a note to those who had not been chosen, saying how much he needed their leadership in winning the Big Opportunity but not, at least right then, on the GC.

The GC began its work with a two-day offsite meeting. It functioned without a formal leader, though a facilitator led this and subsequent meetings and conference calls. An earlier version of the material in chapters 1 and 2 of this book was presented and discussed. A variety of engagement and team-building exercises were employed. The opportunity statement was discussed. Davidson made an appearance. He thanked them for their willingness to take actions that could make a big difference for the organization.

There were many inquiries at first. What exactly do we do? How do we do it? What is the schedule? Who is in charge? To a degree, an explanation of a dual system helped. To a degree, case studies, like the one presented in this chapter, helped. But it was impossible, I think, to explain clearly to people how something they had never experienced before really might work. So the emphasis on the first of those two days was placed on a simple message: you get the chance to make a real difference to this organization in a strategically important way. We know this can be done because other groups like you, at other firms, have done so.

Not surprisingly, there was initial awkwardness about the range of formal statuses represented on the GC, since junior and senior people were working alongside each other. But with the right type of tone and interaction, a new, more fluid and meritocratic, organizational logic began (slowly) to arise: for any given activity in the network, the people with the best information, connections, motivation, and skills took the lead—not necessarily the person with the highest position in the hierarchy.

ACCELERATOR 3: A CHANGE VISION AND STRATEGIC INITIATIVES

Once the GC was formed, its first order of business was to develop a draft change vision for their work and a list of potential strategic initiatives they might focus on, with help from many other volunteers. Their logic was straightforward: the more they could envision where they were going, the better; the more they could focus on specific endeavors to make that vision a reality, the better; the more everything was aligned with the Big Opportunity statement, the better. With input from top management, the outside study Davidson had commissioned, and colleagues throughout the organization, their vision statement read roughly like this:

Within twelve months, the field organization will be gaining market share for the first time in years by:
(1) using intermediaries much more successfully than we

ever have; (2) growing in emerging markets at twice the rate we are today; (3) developing a totally new discipline around innovation in all we do; and (4) making important decisions in half the time we do today (so no longer one month but two weeks, for example). We will employ a proud, passionate group of people and continue gaining momentum to make us the most admired sales organization and the best place to work in the industry.

When this vision statement was shown to the members of the sales executive committee, one or two of them may have written it off as fluff, but most found it refreshingly bold. They loved the fact that people in their organization were committing to big goals—and were doing so voluntarily.

The GC then took a first pass at identifying strategic initiatives that would help achieve the vision and capitalize on the Big Opportunity. From an initial list of nearly twenty, they agreed on five that people wanted most to work on, including attracting and hiring outstanding employees with Asian experience (a tough problem throughout their industry, as good people with such experience were in high demand and short supply) and making the product-introduction process faster and more efficient (an increasingly pressing issue because of the shorter product life cycles and some sales-versus-engineering frictions left over from the firm's early days).

The list of initiatives was given to the sales executive committee, which was generally enthusiastic. They discussed alignment—among the hierarchy's operating plan, its own special projects, the consulting report, the Big Opportunity, the change vision, and the new right side's strategic initiatives—and decided there were no obvious problems. But they worried that the GC might be taking on too much too fast. The GC discussed this advice at what had become their biweekly teleconference, extended the timetable for one of their initiatives, and went to work.

In holding the traditional hierarchy and the new network together, the relationship between the GC and the sales executive committee turned out to be vital yet tricky. At first, the sales executive committee put the GC on its meeting schedule squashed between much routine left-side activity (such as a specific problem with a big customer or a project management report about setting up two offices in Asia). The result was inevitable: the GC was treated like one more piece of left-side business, like one more group of employees reporting to the bosses, in a process that resembled an inquisition more than a dialogue. Motivation flagged. The free flow of communication slowed and interactions became more cautious. But someone spotted the problem and spoke up.

Davidson sought coaching to help clarify how his executive committee and the GC should interact. With help, both groups learned they needed to talk regularly to keep aligned. The executive committee also learned more about its role in this new system—which was mostly to model what was needed from the hierarchy to allow the network to grow and contribute. Davidson learned more about his role too—which was to lead this effort, not manage it or try to take over as the boss of the GC. He found that simple role modeling from him was essential—which meant cheering the GC's successes and treating it as a partner and not a traditional task force.

As a result of the coaching, the whole interaction and relationship between the GC and the sales executive committee changed—not overnight, but it changed. The speed and candor of communication between the groups shifted dramatically. And then motivation within the GC skyrocketed—mostly because they could see that the stage was being set for them to at least have the chance to help the sales organization in a strategically important way.

ACCELERATORS 4 AND 5: ATTRACTING VOLUNTEERS, DRIVING INITIATIVES

How does a GC take a change vision and the resulting strategic initiatives to the entire field organization? In this case, it extended and amplified the original urgency team's methods, using training, communication tools, the portal, and face-to-face conversations, with the latter proving to be particularly powerful. The more team members talked to colleagues, the more people began to be drawn into the whole experience—at first the more curious or adventurous "early adopters," then some who became "the early majority." I was at one lunch where a GC member spoke, and as the group broke up, the man next to me chuckled and quietly said, "For the first time ever, I understand where we need to go, and how. And it actually makes sense!"

Six months into its one-year term, the GC had five major initiatives in place, each of which had one or more sub-initiatives. The move to hire excellent people in Asia, for example, sprouted a sub-initiative to bring new people up to speed more quickly. Those on the subteam asked themselves: what was keeping this from happening? The resulting focus, in much of their work, was on eliminating barriers to accelerated movement in the right direction.

The teams talked, e-mailed, and met as needed to get the work done. In the biweekly GC teleconference, members reported progress, shared information, solicited ideas, and asked for help ("Who has experience with the Japanese market?"). Senior management members of the GC helped to ensure that lower-level employee members received the executive-level information they needed to make sensible decisions, to reduce any tendency toward a seat-of-the-pants mode of operating and avoid the perception that the GC might be a case of "the inmates running the asylum." Lower-level people added front-line information that ordinarily wouldn't have made it up the hierarchy to the executive committee (or would have made it at glacial speed). One big result: the number of little innovative ideas folded into the process grew and grew—and, as a consequence, today two people on the sales executive committee call the strategy-accelerator network "the employee innovation network."

Davidson's early-stage dual operating system

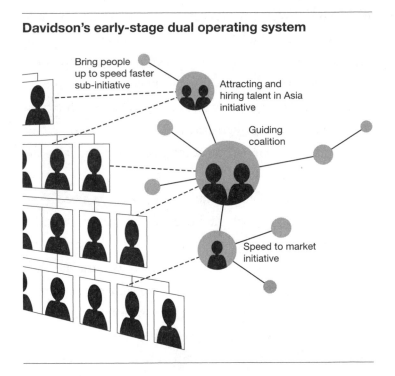

Another big consequence: all of the successful activity attracted another hundred-plus volunteers into the new networked system.

Interestingly, much of the work, they found, was less about finding or generating brand-new good ideas than about knocking down the barriers to making those ideas a reality. It became clear that creative solutions allowing faster movement to capitalize on opportunities had been hidden all over the place—sometimes buried in the hierarchy and invisible to Davidson's executive committee, sometimes inside heads which had been taught not to speak up, or within people who assumed it was not their place to offer thoughts that went way beyond the scope of their "jobs." Everyone involved in the growing network became more question driven, but in a constructive sense. What are the best ideas? Why hasn't this good idea been recognized and executed? What are the barriers? How can we overcome them? What systems or people or cultural assumptions are blocking action? Who will do what by when? How did that turn out? What should we try next?

The barriers they faced in that first year included the fact—which is clear only in retrospect—that the most powerful person reporting to Davidson hated the whole idea of a dual system, the Big Opportunity, volunteers, and a GC. He had a dozen logical concerns and could see no way that they could be addressed. For example, he had no system to keep track of all that was going on with the new volunteer-led initiatives. With strong performance pressures on his part of the organization, he worried constantly that poor decisions and actions, even if taken by well-intentioned people, would create distractions, waste time, and make it impossible for him to hit an aggressive revenue plan. As a result, he did nothing to help the network side, pulled his people off initiatives to do their "real jobs," and never gave any of his people credit for providing a 150% effort—not even so much as a congratulatory e-mail when something new and useful was accomplished outside his group's operating plan. When he saw openings, he also had informal conversations with his peers in which he constantly raised questions about the risks they were taking with this new system.

But, as it turns out, his people (with one possible exception) did not shirk their regular jobs. Why? Those of his people involved in the strategy-accelerator network felt passionate about the work and, as a result, had the energy to do their jobs and then some. Bad decisions did not undermine his short-term goals. Why? The breadth of data that went into decisions, across silos and from all levels in the hierarchy, meant that bad decisions were astonishingly rare. Then network-side "wins" began to impress him. And he could begin to see signs of morale improving in his group because some of his people were so enthusiastic about what they were doing for the company.

Predictably, in driving initiatives, people initially made mistakes. One team launched two small initiatives without first checking to see if similar activities were already in progress in the left-side hierarchy. They were: in one case to redo a section of the contracts being signed with new intermediaries, in the other to reword some details in the statement of their value proposition used in a head-to-head competition against their number 2 market leader. When some of the regular management and staff on the left learned of the initiatives, they became very defensive and territorial. The resulting mayhem wasted time and resources, and strained relationships. But the people in the strategy network learned fast and instituted a simple protocol to make sure that never happened again.

ACCELERATORS 6–8: WINS, WINS, AND MORE WINS

The network organization quickly began to build up lots of small wins, which grew and grew in number and magnitude of impact over time. Then, about six months into the process, came the first big, visible win: a new, simplified IT sales tool was created and implemented at a very low cost in a short period of time.

IT had been a trouble spot for the field organization. Their systems had certainly not been helping increase revenue growth and, in fact, were probably doing the opposite—frustrating employees and wasting time that should have gone into making sales calls. Data entry was cumbersome and time consuming, and the real-time reports were not producing the information sales reps wanted most. An initiative team interviewed users to understand why the system was failing. Then it reached out to potential volunteers from the original list of two thousand who had "raised their hands" as a result of the urgency activities. One e-mail request for help, sent to a hundred people—some of them IT experts in the sales group but most of them not—elicited thirty-five positive responses within four days. Twenty of those people met in a teleconference within two weeks.

The biggest obstacle they encountered in building a new tool was neither technical nor economic but hierarchical, within the IT department. A small group of people worried that they would be blamed for not having already created a tool the salespeople liked. At first they said they were in the process of developing something new and did not need help. Then they raised the question of whether there really was a problem or whether the salespeople were simply misusing their current system. But the initiative team applied what some of their members had learned either through education in the dual-system process or through painful experience. Be unfailingly respectful. Always remember that these bumps are normal, due to human nature and the way hierarchies work. In this case, they kept making the point to all who asked that the overworked IT staff did not have the bandwidth to develop the next-generation tool. And I think they simply wore the resistance down.

A diverse group of highly engaged people—individuals who did not normally have a mechanism to meet, much less want to meet, including front-line salespeople, IT professionals, sales management, and finance staff—had conversations that produced one new idea after another. Tests would show that many of the concepts were impractical. But a few ideas were very clever. They piloted completely new software—running on tablets—that had been built by programmers on the team. Salespeople and their managers loved the end product and rolled it out across the entire field organization. Crucially, the team driving the change made sure that praise was shared all around—in particular, with IT staff and management.

Success with this single, big effort, seen by nearly everyone in the organization, boosted the network's credibility and accelerated progress on other key strategic initiatives. More people joined the accelerator network, showed leadership, became proactive, and were relentless, simply never giving up in the face of barriers

Wins over time

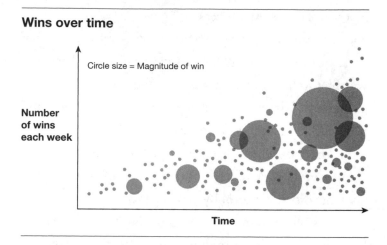

because they could see what could be accomplished. It became impossible to keep track of how many small initiatives were completed in the GC's one-year tenure, but one sub-initiative tried, producing graphs like the one shown here.

Of course many mistakes occurred along the way. But the system continued to improve, and version 4.0 of the GC, in operation as I write this, is without a doubt more sophisticated than ever. It evolves, growing larger and stronger.

The biggest accomplishments so far have been institutionalized in the left side and integrated in daily operations. In cases in which strategic changes didn't fit some aspect of the company culture, the relevant team looked for ways to nurture changes in that culture. To a large extent this happens naturally if the new approach produces better results; but sometimes changes were so big that nurturing was needed.

THE RESULTS SPEAK FOR THEMSELVES

After two years, the results of employing a dual operating approach in responding to their biggest strategic challenges were dramatic—much stronger than Davidson's boldest expectations:

- The system accelerated the creation of new partnerships by 55%. It advanced new ways of dealing with direct customers, a faster product-introduction process, shorter response times on complaints, superior data for the product development group on shifting customer needs, and faster revenue growth in Asia—the latter up by more than 60% in 2011, compared with a 25% increase two years before.

- Sales growth accelerated by 44%. The division started to win back market share so fast that it went from the number 4 player to number 2 in its industry in two years.

- The revenue spurt combined with reduced expense levels helped boost operating income by slightly over 300%.

- The financial community rewarded the overall firm with a 155% increase in market capitalization to over $10 billion (an irrationally large amount, but sometimes that's what happens . . .).

- The firm's reputation as an exciting place to work went from good to great, with the logical implications for recruiting top talent.

No one—inside or outside the firm—would have predicted that these results were even possible when Davidson's organization began developing its new way of operating. But is that at all surprising? No one had a frame of reference for thinking about where the field organization had naturally evolved in its reasonably short life cycle and the inevitable consequences of that evolution. No one had seen a mature organization build a dual system where today's work is done reliably and efficiently while an integrated accelerator network mobilizes an army to deal with strategic challenges quickly and at no extra cost.

EVIDENCE TO DATE FROM OTHER CASES

Davidson's firm is but one case. I and my colleagues have witnessed other pioneering efforts which have also shown dramatic results:

- One federal government organization that was—for due cause—a target for being shut down instead accelerated to become a model facility.

- An energy business that had not grown in years—and had no systems or processes to handle even modest growth, much less any capability to deal with rapid growth or to take advantage of new market opportunities—managed to double its size and capacity within a period of three years.

- A pharmaceutical organization with a considerable growth opportunity in the launch of a few new highly promising products was able to achieve its three-year growth goal within one year.

- A medical products company created enough urgency around a clear opportunity that it essentially went from 60 to 90 miles an hour within only six months. (Financial analysts saw this and rewarded the firm with an irrationally high boost in market capitalization.)

- A moderately large organization within the US military whose fundamental methods for operating had changed little in decades, but which was under great pressure to make some very big

strategic changes, managed in eighteen months
to vastly increase efficiency and capacity, to meet
its new mission, and to institutionalize a new network organization that could continue to help it
meet new demands instead of, once again, becoming stuck in the past.

- The supply-chain organization in a global consumer products business—which had used all of
the modern quality management and lean manufacturing techniques to improve its efficiency and
global capacity, but whose improved results had
flattened out—began, within an eighteen-month
period, to accelerate dramatic strategic shifts and
new productivity gains that surprised executives,
managers, and employees.

- A professional service organization in the world
of finance, despite being very conservative, was
able to increase its market capitalization by 65%
over a twenty-month period (this just three years
after industry analysts had predicted it could be
bought at a bargain price and sliced and diced out
of existence).

In virtually all of these cases, the system that produced dramatic results for the executive vice presidents,
admirals, CEOs, and directors of marketing did not

evaporate after a victory celebration but has sustained itself. In only one of these cases has the left-side hierarchy succeeded in limiting the new accelerator network to a minor role. In the rest, the new fast and agile entrepreneurial capacity has continued to evolve and produce accelerated, profitable growth and other lasting benefits.

SIX

RELENTLESSLY DEVELOPING AND ROLE MODELING URGENCY

Change is not easy. We all know that. Larger-scale, strategically important change can be horrendously challenging. Although we often talk about this challenge in terms of specifics—changing the go-to-market strategy, the global HR IT system, the organizational structure in a key division, important policies or products—the core problem always is about people. People don't want to reorganize, so they don't think clearly about what is needed or pay attention to competent recommendations from others. They use their conventional process, which selects and implements the new global HR IT system too slowly and expensively. They think current policies and products are just fine when, in fact, they are not.

It is not too difficult to see a part of the problem here. Habits keep us doing what we always do. We resist being pushed in new directions that make no sense to us. We cling tenaciously to what we value and fear might be lost. To behave otherwise is somehow less than human.

But there are also less visible forces at play, and in many ways they are much more powerful because they are *systemic*. We identify with people—Fred, who seems to not like anything new, and middle management, which acts like a gigantic rock when we try to deal with a galloping strategic challenge. It is hard to see, much less identify with, a system—in this case a management-driven hierarchy.

A management-driven hierarchy, built for reliability and efficiency *now,* leans against significant change—and leans hugely against a change as significant as the implementation of a dual operating system. It does so, most fundamentally, because its silos, levels, rules, short-term plans, and narrow jobs systematically create complacency. And group complacency is an almost unbelievably powerful force.

The *only* solution to this problem, which I have seen people use successfully, is to create a force powerful enough to reduce and counteract this formidable systemic inclination to stall large-scale change. Traditional task forces, bonuses, strategic plans, program management groups, or strategy consultants don't come close to creating that force. Only the first Accelerator does—by developing and maintaining a strong sense of urgency, among large groups of people, focused on a Big Opportunity.

The secret sauce for kick-starting acceleration

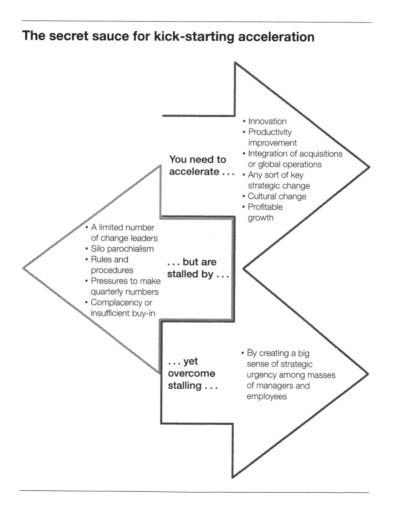

You need to accelerate . . .
- Innovation
- Productivity improvement
- Integration of acquisitions or global operations
- Any sort of key strategic change
- Cultural change
- Profitable growth

. . . but are stalled by . . .
- A limited number of change leaders
- Silo parochialism
- Rules and procedures
- Pressures to make quarterly numbers
- Complacency or insufficient buy-in

. . . yet overcome stalling . . .
- By creating a big sense of strategic urgency among masses of managers and employees

Urgency, in the sense I am using the word here, means that significant numbers of people wake up each morning and have, somewhere in their heads and hearts, a compelling desire to do something to move the organization toward a big strategic opportunity. With aligned energy among enough people, you have a targeted, passionate juggernaut unlike anything found outside wildly successful entrepreneurial firms. The first time you see such a force in action—even in a small firm, much less a large and mature organization—it is breathtaking.

If there is a secret sauce that makes it possible to accelerate and then create a whole new way of running organizations—despite many forces fighting against just that—it is the very first Accelerator.

URGENCY, COMPLACENCY, AND FALSE URGENCY

When people have a true sense of urgency around a big strategic opportunity, they instinctively look for something they can do each day to push the enterprise toward exploiting that opportunity. If that means finding a novel way to communicate the opportunity, and increase urgency in others, they do so. If that means encouraging and celebrating little "wins" that demonstrate faster movement into a successful future, they do it. Their intellectual and emotional commitment to dealing with turbulence and fierce competition shows in their behavior all the time.

Complacency is the opposite orientation. Complacent people see no reason why they should do anything much different. They don't think in terms of looking for ways to develop competitive advantage. Mostly they want to keep doing what they are doing. They may jump on a problem occasionally to keep the firm producing reliable results—and may even appear to have a sense of urgency in doing so. But the problems they tackle tend to be small and not strategic. They tend to be solved in short periods of time, by small groups of people, and with the goal of bringing the system back into an efficient equilibrium.

Well-designed and well-managed hierarchies are good at producing that sort of energy: to fix the machine which has shut down assembly line #4, or to deal with a customer screaming on the phone about poor service, or to complete the report which the boss has suddenly said must be on her desk at 9:00 a.m. Friday. Sometimes people may be running around to meetings and more meetings, or generating reports and more reports, and from a distance this can look like a sense of urgency around important issues. But these actions really represent a kind of anxiety-driven false urgency, which usually produces only self-protective activity rather than productively pushing the organization into a prosperous future.

People never admit to being complacent. No one will tell you that strategic complacency is a good thing. But the world is filled with it, and even the most competent people often don't see it. The system in which they have been raised and in which they operate makes them blind to complacency. From the top of an organization, it can seem so obvious that a big strategic problem or opportunity exists. So a CEO or his or her executives cannot imagine that others do not see the challenge and feel a sense of urgency to deal with it. But they often don't, and for reasons that are very understandable.

For example:

- Your company's market share is crashing, and a turnaround will require some significant changes in marketing strategy, the sales organization, and customer service. This is hardly a secret: the *Wall Street Journal* seems to run an article on some aspect of the situation daily. So top management cannot help but see the proverbial burning platform. Executives with a huge sense of urgency often assume that the same must be true for everyone in the company. But in fact that's far from correct among the many employees who live in a world in which they rush from meeting to meeting dealing with short-term issues and crises, where there is little if any discussion about the *WSJ,* and where most people don't even read the *WSJ.*

- The research group has developed a new technology that offers a big new product opportunity—with the potential to generate growth that could move the firm into first place in its older, B2B industry. But exploiting that research will require five or six significant initiatives in manufacturing—a fact which should be obvious to any manager who thinks about the subject. The CEO thinks a great deal about the subject. Most of middle management within manufacturing has heard about the new technology, some of them more than others. But the pressures on them from their management-driven hierarchy are to get the product out each day and to solve the fifty different problems that threaten to keep the required volume of quality products from rolling out the door each week. For every two-hour meeting top management has on the topic of the new technology—the opportunity it offers, the resources needed to exploit it, and the kinds of initiatives needed in manufacturing—the typical factory manager may spend two minutes dealing with the subject. Those who spend more do it in informal worry sessions. The workers on the floor might spend two seconds.

- Based on an extensive study of events in the past decade, the secretary of the Army is telling a large military unit in Alabama to undergo a fundamental transformation, which will require a major reorganization. The buzz about this problem has been raging throughout the Pentagon and Washington, DC, for months. How is it possible for someone not to hear the buzz? The answer: it is very possible for lots of people outside the in-the-clouds otherworld called the US capital. And as for those within the specific Army unit who do hear the buzz, they have learned that noise in Washington is usually about transitory politics, not enduring reality, so they mostly ignore it. And "noise" it is, since information does not flow easily to people nearly a thousand miles away and many levels below in the bureaucracy.

When confronted with clear evidence that strategic complacency or false urgency is rampant, we often explain it in terms of that frustrating tendency for people to resist change. This could be a part of the problem, but the bigger issue is systemic. That is, a management-driven hierarchy systematically creates competitive complacency, and, when the pressures are great, false urgency. Silos limit access to information about the big picture, and certainly any big-picture opportunities or threats. Narrow job parameters send the message that as long as you are doing your little job today, you are fine.

Managerial processes tend to focus people's attention inward—on the budget, the plan, the staff, and the metrics. This inward focus means a lower probability of seeing external strategic opportunities or threats. Multiple levels in a hierarchy create communication challenges, so even if a few people at the top have a strong sense of urgency about a Big Opportunity, that information rarely reaches the bottom clearly, without distortion, and with the volume required. Managerial processes, often so metrically focused and analytical, cut off an emotional attachment to anything—and with that, the needed energy and passion. A well-functioning left-side machine really doesn't need or want emotion. Feelings, the thinking goes, are not easily managed and can muck up the stable reliability of the system more than help.

In light of all of this, how is it even possible to create a true sense of urgency, within masses of people, about a big strategic opportunity? It is possible. But it requires actions that are far from the norm in most organizations today.

LOOKING OUTWARD, OPEN MINDED

Developing the mega-force of strategic urgency requires, first of all, that people be aware of what's going on around them, think seriously about what it means, and be open to and excited about new possibilities.

Inwardly focused organizations, or inwardly focused silos built within the hierarchies, can be filled with good people who don't see the obvious: that more big changes are happening more quickly outside their enterprises which require them to make big changes inside those enterprises. "Bringing the outside in" means using every possible communication mechanism to import the reality of the situation. An outside-in approach might mean, for example, arranging for external speakers at meetings; sending groups to visit organizations that are facing similar threats or opportunities; selectively hiring people who see and appreciate the true turbulence you face; or highlighting the field intelligence of employees who are in a strong position to see outside (e.g., salespeople who must travel to client sites). There are dozens of ways to bring relevant external realities to the attention of employees and managers.

Creating strategic urgency can mean pointing out external hazards or potential crises. It must mean dialogue about new possibilities and opportunities, which sometimes come about because of a crisis.

So often, people point to crises or potential crises only as a scare tactic. It's a way of hitting people on the head to kill complacency. There are certainly cases in which people need a wake-up call and a blow on the head may be essential. But repeated bashings do not help and do not work. The evidence is overwhelming that once you have people's attention, the presentation of an opportunity is much more likely than a threat or a prediction of doom to increase their energy level to want to do something new. There is no question that the organizations that emerged quickly from the storm of the financial crises of 2008–2009 did so because, in the words of one of my colleagues, they spent less time building shelters and more time building windmills.

Effectively instilling a sense of strategic urgency can mean broadcasting information about what some managers or staff have already done to move toward new opportunities—actions which have achieved some clear and impressive results. The best communication here will not look routine. It will capture people's attention in a way that almost compels them to be open minded. It does so by stating the case in a way that pulls on the emotional strings common to us all. Great communication—no matter the topic—always connects with people's feelings and with what they find meaningful.

A management-driven hierarchy does not even try to connect with feelings. Even if it tries to communicate information about a Big Opportunity, it will have an inclination to do so by making a "business case" for it. The built-in inclination will be to use data and logic to generate urgency around significant change. This method will have an effect. But it will not be enough to build the needed mega-force.

I have yet to see a situation in which a traditional business case has created a massive sense of urgency among large groups of people around a big strategic opportunity. The difficulty is multifold.

First, business cases tend to be complex, especially when they are trying to justify changes in the allocation of significant resources. It is not uncommon for such a business case—in the form of a report from a sophisticated consulting firm—to be 75 to 100 pages long, to be filled with dense data, and to require a verbal presentation to even begin to explain itself. It's not unusual for top management to struggle to understand all the data—and the accompanying logic and justification for the recommended course of action—much less middle management or below. In light of these challenges, such business cases are rarely presented to managers more than once or twice, perhaps over a few hours in a meeting. Think about that. There is no way that any method, applied in such a limited, infrequent way, could create sufficient urgency to lead to significant changes. And that is not even considering the fact that a business case is a purely analytical tool, meant to appeal to rationality and not to feelings.

Possibly the biggest problem of all here is that any case for change can work only if people are willing to listen, and with an open mind. Complacent people will rarely listen unless information comes at them multiple times, and with some emotional pull. They will not listen unless the situation is put into a context that seems relevant to them. Managers and employees who are truly complacent—who think and feel that what they're doing is just fine, thank you—will at best listen to what you are saying with one ear.

Imagine that a truly great car salesman tries to sell you a new, more technologically sophisticated car. But you are satisfied with your current car. Odds are you will cut off the salesman before he can make much of a sales pitch. "Thank you, but. . . ." Perhaps he has cornered you at a party, and you are forced to listen. You may be too polite to walk away. But you will be thinking about how to get away much more than you'll be listening openly to what he has to say—even if he is talking about a superb product and has a ton of data demonstrating that it is a superb product. Forced to listen for an extended period of time, you are more likely to feel annoyed than to develop any sense of true urgency. If you're living in a world of anxiety-driven false urgency, you're more likely to be thinking about the stupid meeting that you must attend at 7:00 the next morning and how you can avoid being corralled into taking on still more work. In either case, your mind is closed.

THE POWER OF ROLE
MODELING URGENCY

Nothing is as powerful in opening masses of minds, supplying relevant information, drawing out passion, and then creating a great sense of urgency around a big competitive opportunity than role modeling. In the successful dual systems I've seen built, such role modeling typically starts at the top. But it can begin anywhere, with anyone, and spread in unpredictable ways. As more and more people role model urgency—where ten people each influence ten others, then those ten each touch ten more—the net result can be an exponential growth of a very powerful force.

When a person role models urgency, he or she starts quite naturally to talk about strategic challenges or possibilities or initiatives in hallway conversations, to bring them up in meetings, to slide them into e-mails, or to insert mentions of them whenever some issue or problem that relates to a Big Opportunity comes up. With regularity and confidence, but not boasting, these individuals tell others what they are actually doing, and why it is important; they do not just tell others what the others should do. It's amazing what communicating sixty seconds here and two minutes there can achieve if it is done consistently, day after day.

Years ago, I met a person who can only be described as an urgency machine. He was in his late thirties, a senior vice president in a high-tech organization based in the United States. During the day I was with him, he inserted into various conversations, at least a dozen times over six hours, some variation of a past-success-guarantees-nothing speech, served up not as an admonishment but rather as an honest reminder of the way the world works. He peppered his conversations with examples here and there of people who were taking actions that could lead the firm toward a huge opportunity. He had a two-paragraph copy of a statement about competitive opportunities, written on a single page, sitting on the conference table in his office, and he almost always referred to it before a meeting ended—the implicit (and sometimes explicit) question being "Are the actions we are discussing aligned with this statement?" He conducted himself in an upbeat way that did not seem manufactured, but totally authentic. He looked for complacency in all his encounters. (I know, because he talked about this with me at the end of the day I spent with him.) One of his subordinates told me over lunch that the man was a "fantastic role model." Of course what defines successful role models is the fact that, over time, others around them start to think and act as they do. And such imitation has deep and lasting impact.

When a leader role models strategic urgency, this is very different than some of the actions taken by managers running hierarchies. A management-driven hierarchy tends to relegate action into its silos. So the communications department might be asked to develop messaging about a strategic opportunity and deliver it to the organization. But the most competent communications group in the world will not have the credibility of a leader who speaks passionately and with authenticity about what he or she is doing to capitalize on strategic issues. Management-driven hierarchies delegate work to the training silo. Despite the competence of the training people, they never have budgets to put masses of people through courses. And even people who may get excited by a message in training will, when back on the job, look around to see if anyone else has picked up the message and is behaving accordingly. Usually what they will see is that very few people have. This can create cynicism more than great urgency around a Big Opportunity.

CREATING POSITIVE ENERGY, CELEBRATING SEIZED OPPORTUNITIES

A large part of the effective and relentless role modeling of urgency is to make visible and celebrate any seized opportunities—even if they are small wins—that demonstrate movement in a strategically sensible and exciting direction. Wins give credibility to the whole idea of pursuing a new strategic advantage. Celebrations give a needed pat on the back to people who are trying to help. The emotional reward of these pats is positive energy, which not only makes an individual feel good but also has a cumulative effect within the organization. I think we have all seen how powerful such energy can be.

You sometimes see such leadership and positive energy in a management-driven hierarchy. But they are rare, and for good reasons. Management-driven hierarchies are designed to offer either economic rewards or threats. When strategic plans are created, the same methods are applied. Carrots and sticks. With economic carrots, you give managers new goals, only achievable if they implement a new strategy; make sure there are measures in place to track whether they are meeting the goals; and then reward them with money when they do. This approach is based on the belief that economic carrots can drive hearts and minds in creating action. To some degree this is true—but only up to a point. And to how many people in an organization can you offer significant economic incentives? Usually only a small percentage.

Sticks come in a variety of forms. Pressure from the top is the most common. The message is simple: this is what you have to do, and if you don't. . . . Far too often this approach inadvertently creates false urgency—that anxiety-driven set of activities which might look impressively busy and productive but which achieves little for an organization. It can even generate anger, which can be converted into the equivalent of an insurgency. This might take the form of a very creative passive resistance through which people find a thousand excuses for why the action that the boss needs is not happening: the IT guys are late; the resources provided are insufficient; sudden problems with customer X had to be fixed; and so on ad nauseam.

Both carrots and sticks come from the outside, and they are controlled and defined by others. Useful small wins can be defined by the people taking early action themselves, and they can provide intrinsic rewards. Consider, for instance, a financial analyst who succeeds in pulling the eight people in her office area into the urgency realm. It is a big shift in their orientation and may seem "nice" to senior management, if they even hear about it. But this sort of shift hardly meets an executive standard for a "win." Yet for the analyst, whose complacent coworkers were driving her crazy, this success could be huge, providing a feeling of accomplishment and increased motivation that is hard to adequately quantify.

Multiply the success of that one analyst, and the accompanying motivation and confidence, by 10 or 50 or 500 and you have a very powerful force. It is a force created by what are essentially many small acts of leadership, relentlessly role modeling urgency around rapidly moving strategic opportunities.

ANYTIME, ANYWHERE, ANYONE

Being relentless is key. This means role modeling with as many mechanisms as possible, as often as possible, and involving as many people as possible.

Jack McGovern travels regularly as a part of his senior management job at a Midwest heavy-metal manufacturing company. His last trip included four stops in the United States, three stops in Europe, one in the Middle East, and four in Asia. During this tour, with no additional time allocation on his schedule for "communication of strategic issues," he found ways to speak to people on at least twenty-five occasions about—and visibly demonstrate through his actions—his own sense of urgency around big challenges facing the enterprise.

In Frankfurt, on the spur of the moment, he gathered about twenty people for a luncheon in which he gave an impromptu talk about his view of the firm's biggest opportunity and its importance, all delivered with a passion that accurately reflected how he felt. In London, he ended all of his meetings by passing out a copy of a statement from the executive committee about creating competitive advantage, along with some written commentary that he had added, all still fitting on one page. Passing out the page and commenting on it required about five minutes. In Shanghai, where he gave a speech to about a hundred people, somewhere during the talk he started spontaneously telling his audience about how the firm had this huge opportunity, how he was thinking about it, and what he thought some of the initiatives might be that could help them exploit it. In Los Angeles, he put his one-page sheet on bulletin boards, whenever he saw one, probably adding up to two dozen postings over his two-day visit. In Chicago, when he bumped into a person who was on what was called the firm's "urgency team," he spent a few minutes, over a cup of coffee, asking what the man was doing and showing his obvious excitement and pleasure over some of those actions.

Jurgen Bandarhouse is a classic geek who has taken visible leadership in creating an "urgency portal" for his firm. It started out rather simply as a basic website. When more and more people were drawn into this activity by Jurgen's enthusiasm and successes, it grew. It now accepts news from anyone in the firm. It has videos shot by many people—almost all very informal, some silly, some very informative—showing what people are doing after having developed a sense of urgency around a big strategic initiative. People post blogs. The executive committee's "Big Opportunity statement" is prominent, along with a series of ongoing conversations on the statement itself among people around the firm. The portal was initially buried somewhere within another portal that was in turn buried within another website.

The executive committee is now considering putting it on everyone's home page.

Molly Halbert has developed a game, played on the computer, which is wildly innovative and fun. Instead of being about winning a hand of poker, it's about finding the biggest strategic challenges and opportunities in a mythical kingdom. Wen Dalton, working with a team of people, has developed a small kit which can be given to supervisors who would like guidance in how to talk about strategic challenges with their teams. Another young person, who in her day job is an actuary, but who apparently has had a lifelong dream of being a Hollywood filmmaker, has become a leading force in giving assistance to anyone in the firm producing short videos, usually two to four minutes long, that help with the urgency effort. The videos are sent through e-mails, put on the urgency portal, and shown at meetings. Some, quite frankly, aren't very good, but they are always authentic. Some are highly interesting and entertaining.

When people who have a sense of urgency around a big strategic opportunity are turned loose and told that they can be as innovative as possible in drawing more and more of their colleagues in, it is amazing what I've seen happen. They tend to do it as a night job because they think it is important, fun, or interesting. Not all that they do is particularly impactful. But when you add it all up, it makes a big difference, especially because successful ventures draw more people in, some of whom create additional successful ventures of their own. And so the momentum builds.

This activity certainly works best when no one tries to project manage it. That means it is not carefully controlled. That means there may be no one in senior management who can list even 5% of the activity that's going on. This will make some managers who are highly trained in a left-side, management-driven hierarchy nervous at first. But it works.

And it creates a passionate energy that is difficult to imagine unless you have seen it. It is a force that beats everything else in overcoming a hierarchy's inherent resistance to creating a dual system, immediately attacking a strategic challenge, and accelerating into the future. The force grows, to a large extent, from the excitement that builds around a "Big Opportunity"— the latter being an integral piece, to which I will turn in the next chapter.

SEVEN

THE BIG OPPORTUNITY

Great urgency that drives people in a dozen different directions achieves nothing.

The energy that is at the core of accelerated action and dual operating systems is an *aligned* energy. The kind of pioneers who create these systems begin by developing not just a powerful sense of strategic urgency among large numbers of people, but a force for change that aligns people's feelings, thoughts, and actions.

Alignment means group focus, and that begs the question: Focus on *what:* In order to build the momentum needed to overcome a management-driven hierarchy's tendency toward stability? To overcome the forces that stall any inclination to leap into a new way of operating with speed and agility? To get the most people moving as quickly as possible?

You could begin the process by aligning on strategic goals. Another alternative would be to align on a vision. Or a set of strategic initiatives. Or more specific plans.

ACCELERATE

Ultimately all of these possibilities need to be comparable so as to build momentum in the same direction. But at the start, what do you need to build urgency around? Or does it really matter, as long as the energy that develops is aligned?

In the most successful cases of accelerating a new strategy and building a dual system, it does seem to matter a great deal. And in terms of vision or strategy or strategic initiatives or plans, the answer regarding the best place to begin is: *none of the above.* There is another alternative which, for a number of reasons, is much better.

THE PLACE TO START: POSSIBILITIES AND OPPORTUNITY

Almost all highly performing organizations have in their futures the possibility of continuing to prosper greatly despite moving into a world where the rules have changed. There are very few solid enterprises that do not have the potential to go from good to great, and very few struggling organizations that cannot stop struggling and start winning. Of course, when it comes to big change, threats are usually more visible. But change always brings with it new possibilities and opportunities.

As I use the term here, a "Big Opportunity" is usually the product of changes in an organization's environment

132

(such as new markets, new advances in technology, or new demands being placed on an enterprise by competition or turmoil), changes inside the organization (such as new products or new people), or both. A Big Opportunity is something that can potentially lead to significant outcomes if the possibility is exploited well enough and fast enough. These outcomes might include much-accelerated profitable growth; the power to innovate much faster in a world that demands more innovation; a much better (and well-deserved) reputation that draws talent and financial resources your way as never before; or the accomplishment of an ambitious mission to serve people, communities, and country.

A Big Opportunity is both rational in light of available data and emotionally compelling to people inside an organization. It draws on both the heart and the mind. A well-articulated statement of a Big Opportunity compellingly describes a window to the future that is open or is about to open. With the right framing and application, the statement makes the people involved excited about jumping through that window.

Increasingly such windows are appearing, opening, and closing much more quickly than ever before. Twenty years ago, much less forty or sixty, these windows of strategic opportunity might have stayed open for ten years or more. Now they can disappear in a fraction of that time. There was no need to race to set up a significant presence in China, Indonesia, or Brazil a few decades ago because the markets for most products and services there were minuscule or unavailable to outsiders. Today a great many of these markets are significant, active, and growing at 20% per year.

A Big Opportunity is *not* a "vision," although the two may seem similar. A Big Opportunity could be, in part, "Because of contextual factor X and our special capability Y, we have a very real and exciting opportunity to offer service Z and substantially grow our revenues and profits starting in this year and continuing on for at least five years, with unprecedented benefits flowing from the top of the firm to the bottom." If decision-making speed, customer service, and talent are three of the key issues that will need to be changed for a firm to capture this opportunity, a one-year change vision could be, in part, "We will be making decisions faster, serving our customers' needs better, and be a place where people want to work, feeling great pride in what they do."

People who create successful dual systems center the creation of great urgency around opportunity, not vision, for two basic reasons. First, in traditional hierarchies, managers and other employees look at any commentary about the future through the lens of their silos, or their sub-silos. The more any initial statement paints a picture of what those silos will look like in the future (which visions by nature often do), the greater the odds that some people will see something in the statement they do not like, because it might seem to them to shrink their silos' power, influence, budget, or other resources. The result will be a negative reaction and active or passive resistance. Opportunity statements do not elicit the same sort of reaction, or at least do so much less frequently, because of the focus on logical and exciting possibilities outside an organization, not explicit or implicit threats to people's status, power, options, or very existence inside an organization.

Second, vision statements can easily have the tone of "this is our vision and you will make it happen." Top management rarely means to communicate in this fashion, but that is how it is heard. Some people don't mind the tone because at least the bosses seem to know where the enterprise needs to go. Or they don't mind because they greatly respect the CEO. But in general vision statements, as a vehicle to build urgency, all too easily make people feel as if they are being talked down to, and—big surprise—they don't like being treated in a way that feels threatening or condescending. Bottom line: this makes people *stop* when you need them to *go*. A well-crafted statement of a Big Opportunity sounds less like a finger pointed inward at the managerial and employee children and more like a finger pointed outward at a rainbow.

A Big Opportunity is also *not* any form of "strategy" or "strategic initiative." A strategy is usually just a more analytical way of describing a vision. A great vision is literally something that one can imagine visually: it is about actions, people, customers—and therefore what businesses you wish to be in. A good strategy uses numbers and logic to justify what businesses you should be in, where you should be positioned in those businesses, and key policies that will let you win with that positioning. "Strategic initiatives" tend to be arenas in which action needs to be taken to move an organization toward a change vision, or to implement a strategy. If the vision and strategy call for a major transformation to take advantage of the opportunity, then all the strategic initiatives will need to add up to create that transformation.

Both of the problems with relentlessly creating urgency first around a vision also apply to strategy and strategic initiatives. Both can easily be seen by people in silos as threatening their status or resources, and both can seem to fall out of the sky as orders from above. In addition, strategies and strategic plans usually come out sounding complex to people with narrowly defined jobs—which means just about everyone. People can struggle to comprehend complex documents, and some of them will resent deeply, if only unconsciously, being made to feel stupid. People who feel stupid will often act like a mule: they will stubbornly refuse to move. A well-crafted Big Opportunity statement can be comprehended by a clerk or a factory worker—and has the potential to create a true sense of urgency in the offices, in the factories, or anywhere.

If you start with strategies or strategic initiatives to create aligned urgency, more often than not you will be

---

The Big Opportunity begets a change vision, which begets strategic initiatives

The Big Opportunity
A window into a winning future that is realistic, emotionally compelling, and memorable

⬇

Change vision
What you need to look like to be able to capitalize on the Big Opportunity

⬇

Strategic initiatives
Activities that, if designed and executed fast enough and well enough, will make your vision a reality

---

using statements that are emotionally barren: all head and no heart. Exceptionally few people are hooked—in terms of strong positive feelings of urgency, with all the positive power that comes with them—if an idea is all head and no heart. Once again, the net result is that the number of people who will want to do something new, make something new happen—want to *go*—can be very, very small. With well-thought-out Big Opportunity statements, however, the opposite is true—and that is crucial to kick-start the whole process of accelerated strategy execution, adjustment, and the launching of a dual system.

The point here is not that the strategy work done in virtually all mature organizations today should be ignored or discarded if you want to accelerate strategic action and build a dual system. Hardly. Sometimes a strategic plan can be the force that helps launch an effort to create urgency around an opportunity (which is what happened in Davidson's case in chapter 5). At a minimum, it must be taken into account when a Big Opportunity statement is created, because if the two are not aligned, you will be set on a course from day one in which the hierarchy and network parts of a dual system will struggle to work together as one organization. The point is that taking existing strategic plans, perhaps condensing them to make them easier to communicate, and then using them as the starting point to build aligned urgency usually does not work well, for all the reasons listed above.

CREATING THE
"BIG OPPORTUNITY" STATEMENT

The most effective Big Opportunity statement seems to have these characteristics. It is:

- **Short.** It can be written on less than a page, often just a quarter of a page. Its length makes it easier to share with others and thus easier to create a sense of urgency around it among large groups of people.

- **Rational.** It makes sense in light of real happenings inside and outside an organization. A reasonable person will not reject the Big Opportunity statement (let's now call it TBO for shorthand) because it sounds like a fantasy based on an inaccurate assessment of reality. A good TBO often addresses issues of *what, why, why us, why now,* and *why bother,* all in a short statement.

- **Compelling.** It also is somehow emotionally compelling. It is not all head. There is heart in it. And it speaks to the hearts of all relevant audiences— not just to people at the bottom of the hierarchy or the top, to some silos and not others.

- **Positive.** Because it is about an opportunity, it has a positive tone. It is less like a statement about a "burning platform," which seeks to scare us out of our complacency, and more like a statement of a "burning desire."

- **Authentic.** It feels real. It is not just "good messaging" that might motivate the troops. The senior leadership team that puts it together, or at least signs off on it, genuinely believes it and feels excited about it.

- **Clear.** You can create a statement that is short, rational, emotionally compelling . . . but still unclear. A lack of clarity will always, at some point, undermine the development of a dual system, as people rush off in nonaligned directions.

- **Aligned.** An effective TBO is aligned with any existing similar statements, and thus dual systems, at higher levels in an organization. If a firm already has a dual system operating at the firm level, but the engineering organization wants to create its own new system to deal with huge and strategically important engineering issues, the engineering TBO must be aligned with the corporate statement. More broadly, any lack of alignment with existing documents (e.g., strategic plans) will eventually create stresses and strains.

Here's a simple summary that covers virtually all the points: A TBO must be *rational* (why us, why now, why . . .), *emotionally compelling* (a sincere, positive, authentic appeal to the heart), and *memorable* (clear, short, no jargon).

One of the reasons that vision and mission statements, as so often created these days, fail to have any useful effect on an organization is that they lack these qualities. So they are hard for others to understand, seem like fluff instead of sensible analysis, simply feel inauthentic, or are not compelling enough to influence behavior. Therefore they elicit the *stop* response.

I have found that successful TBOs are created by the executive team of the unit that wants (1) a strategy accelerated immediately, (2) a new way of operating to win in a twenty-first-century world, or (3) both. The unit could be a firm, a division of a firm, a functional or geographical entity within a firm, a nonprofit organization (such as a school system), or a part of some governmental organization (such as a piece of the Navy). We have no evidence that consultants or task forces can write this sort of statement for the people who actually run the relevant unit.

Although there could be templates for what a TBO should precisely look like, and thus creating one could be a matter of just filling in the blanks, I have seen no evidence that this is true. People appear to need some space in terms of content and process to make the statement truly right for them.

I have found that the key to creating great TBOs is to have total clarity about your goals. The most fundamental are:

1. To create a statement which is memorable, smart, and emotionally compelling.

2. To have a product so good that, when top management is asked if they believe in it, and if they want deeply to take advantage of it, everyone in the room will raise their hands, most of them quickly and with total sincerity.

3. To have a statement so good that a few on the executive committee want to help take it to the rest of their organization in order to create a great sense of urgency around that opportunity. When at least two people on the executive committee truly volunteer to help lead the effort—not even knowing exactly what they are volunteering for, how much time it might take, or the difficulty of the task—then you have a good indicator that you have achieved the task of creating a great TBO.

EXAMPLE: RAPID GROWTH IN MANUFACTURING SERVICES

The firm was based on the East Coast of the United States. When we worked with it, the enterprise had revenues of $7 billion a year. Its business was building manufacturing facilities for other firms. Its industry had been stagnant globally for over a decade. A number of forces—economic, social, and political—were all coming together to change that reality, quite possibly in a very big way. The senior leadership team knew this, but they asked a task force to look at the data more formally and report back to them. The task force reported that the opportunity, in their judgment, was indeed huge.

The executive committee developed, then used to create a sense of urgency, a TBO. Half of the leadership team embraced the statement with an energy level and sense of urgency not seen in the firm for many years. Most of them had hated their "time in the desert" (their phrase), when the industry and their revenue growth had been stagnant. Most of the rest of the team thought the statement was quite possibly true. They certainly hoped it was valid, but its accuracy was not guaranteed—and thus they were both intellectually and emotionally guarded. One team member looked on the Big Opportunity with a cynical sneer ("I've heard this before . . .")—a sentiment which, however, he would not share with the CEO in the room.

This, and all the examples that follow, are disguised. But the essentials of the organizational contexts and statements are kept. In this case, the statement read as follows:

Because of changing attitudes among the public and shifting marketplace needs, we have the opportunity to double our revenues within four or five years and to become the leading global company in our industry. That would mean the leading firm in terms of market share in those areas where we compete. That would mean the highest percentage of new plants that are built.

This possibility is realistic as long as we maintain our leadership in technology, which is most certainly possible. This is realistic if we live our values every day, which we can.

Our success, ultimately, will come because of our customers' success. And our successful customers will help millions of people around the globe to have better lives.

Most of us have seen statements like this that seem, at first glance, to be rhetorical fluff, and which ultimately achieve nothing useful. These communiqués are sent in an e-mail or read at a meeting. They are carved into plaques that hang on walls in some offices or plants. They achieve little for a number of reasons. But the one here worked. Why?

In this case, some of the employees who had heard pronouncements over the years that good days were just around the corner, when in fact they were not, did at first react cautiously or outright cynically to the statement. But younger people did not. Those who so wanted the statement to be true did not. Those who saw the stars aligning did not. Most of the executive committee who created this statement did not. Therefore, the TBO had the potential to be a powerful vehicle for generating a sense of aligned urgency among many people and putting them into *go* mode. It had the potential to overcome the strategic complacency and fogginess that are built into hierarchies.

And in this case that potential was maximized because, just as outlined in chapter 6, people, starting with the executive committee and then going far beyond, were relentless in communicating this idea, through deeds and words. Accelerator number 1 worked as it was supposed to. A powerful force was created to begin the process of strategy acceleration and the building of a dual operating system.

EXAMPLE: REVOLUTIONIZING SUPPLY CHAINS

Consider another company, this time in high tech, located on the West Coast, and with about $2 billion in yearly revenues. In its traditional product areas, it was third in market share. But its industry was going through a discontinuity in which a radically new technology threatened to make existing product lines obsolete. There was much uncertainty.

Here is its TBO:

Customers are rethinking their entire supply-chain infrastructure. We have the opportunity to revolution-ize supply-chain processes with our innovative products and our culture of people who are so highly dedicated to customer success. We have a very realistic opportunity to become the first choice of customers and to build a com-pany that we can be proud of for the rest of our lives.

Here is a statement even shorter than the previous one. But look at what is packed into just three sentences. A major assessment of what exactly they could do for cus-tomers (revolutionize their supply-chain processes). A very specific belief about the epicenter for those changes (in their supply-chain infrastructure). A belief that the firm can use new products it judges to be innovative to fundamentally change its customers' supply-chain infra-structure in ways that will help those organizations to succeed. An assessment that with their customer-first cul-ture, their sales force would be able to convince custom-ers, some undoubtedly pretty conservative, to buy those products, even though using them might require some significant changes. An implicit assertion that all this will lead the firm to growing market share ("first choice of customers"). Another implicit belief that this will lead to great pride inside the firm, which would mean a lot to employees and to the future success of the firm.

I could take all of this, connect the dots more carefully, fill in some facts or assumptions with face validity, and have a two- or three-page document that would sound more like a new business strategy. Or throw in more statistics and make it into ten to twenty pages—all of which would be hard to remember, cerebrally complex, emotionally flat, and with sufficient detail to elicit silo- or level-based paranoia in a significant number of people.

This statement is also different from the first example because the change that opens the window of opportunity is technological—not economic, social, and political. But it mostly meets the criteria satisfied by the statement in the first case. And though it may not seem particularly exciting to some readers of this book, that is irrelevant. What is relevant is that it was compelling to the people in that firm.

EXAMPLE: TRANSFORMING SALES AND MARKETING IN HEALTH CARE

Another case. Here the firm is the US unit—almost all sales and marketing people—of a European-based high-tech business in the health space. The parent organization has revenues of $18 billion.

The short story was this. The US leadership team had two potentially huge new products, and they had two huge products ending their life cycle. The budgeting process used by their traditional left-side organization predictably looked at historical precedents inside the firm and projected future scenarios accordingly. Those projections called for a dip in revenues for a few years (because the old products died off faster than the new ones caught on), up to, in the best case scenario, slow increases in revenues for a few years (because the rise of the new products went a bit faster than the death of the old). Because silos (and people) tend to be self-protective in management-driven hierarchies, when up-from-the-bottom budgets were amalgamated, the projected revenue line was flat for three years and the profit line went down. Thus the discussion was all about the problem and not about any bold opportunity—until the division's head of sales and marketing spoke up firmly, and with conviction, to the executive committee.

"Why do we have to launch these two new big products as we have in the past, or with only minor improvements to our standard process? Why don't we act very differently? Yes, that would require some significant transformations in marketing and sales. Yes, that would require a new way of making these strategic transformations. But run the numbers. Look what this could do to revenue growth over two to five years. Look what it would do to our competitive position. Look what it would do for us and our employees. Who wouldn't love winning, winning, winning, instead of holding on as best we can? Our headquarters staff would flip from being all over us all the time to being a huge supporter. And run the numbers on sales commissions!"

Thus started a dialogue, which led to a TBO, then to the building of a new dual system, which created a big payoff even faster than the head of sales and marketing had dreamed.

The unit's Big Opportunity statement:

With our new products, there is no reason that we cannot double the size of the US company in less than five years, resulting in greatly increased commissions for our entire sales force. Our customers will be happy, our sales force will be happy, and our parent organization will be ecstatic!

This is the shortest opportunity statement yet, but again there is a lot of information packed into it. The new products to be released soon are key here. They help address the *what, why now,* and *why us* questions. And, in its own highly concentrated way, the statement speaks to both analytical, data-based criteria ("double the size . . . in less than five years") and the emotions ("ecstatic" and "happy") of people across three integral groups (customers, sales force, parent organization).

I recently showed this specific opportunity statement to someone at another company, and he said: "But we don't have any strategic opportunities of this magnitude.

Anything we wrote that was honest would come out dreary. Or pedestrian." Which, as it turns out, was precisely the way at least half of the executives were originally thinking in the organization which produced the statement reprinted above.

EXAMPLE: CHANGING THE GAME IN THE MILITARY

In this case, the organization was a unit in the US military being asked by Washington to do about 30% more than it had ever done before, or at least since World War II. It had been trying to increase its output using many of the methods pervasively found today: expanded targets in operating plans, special-purpose task forces, rather stern speeches from the commanding general to his top fifty officers. But progress was painfully slow in an organization which had been conducting business pretty much the same way for decades.

Their TBO read as follows:

With the personnel we now have in place at the top of the unit, with the demands being placed upon us by Washington, and with the very real challenges of a continuing war, we now have the opportunity to eliminate inefficient processes and organizational inertia which have built up over fifty years.

We have the opportunity, over the next two years, to create a mindset where there is a new sense of optimism, mission accomplishment, and accountability. This will be a dramatic change in both ideas and practice which will help us meet our immediate goals and better position us to deal with the challenges of the twenty-first century.

We cannot miss this opportunity. We cannot fail our government, our nation, our unit, and our people.

Here, an organization caught in the past had an opportunity to prepare itself for the future by leveraging off very severe and real short-term demands. Before creating this statement, they had previously talked about their situation, at least in private, in very negative ways—unreasonable goals from an out-of-touch and hopelessly politicized Pentagon, for example—and they had used conventional productivity improvement methods, which succeeded up to a point and then were ineffective. They were failing until the leaders recognized the opportunity in the situation and crafted it into a statement that was logical, compelling, and memorable. This led to an entirely different approach, which met their immediate strategic challenge and built a new way of operating for the future.

The first part of the first Accelerator is creating a force that can begin the development of a dual system by

The Big Opportunity, the network, and accelerated results

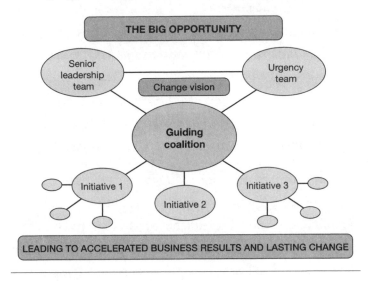

identifying or clarifying a Big Opportunity. Everything flows from there. The second part of that Accelerator is finding the means, as described in chapter 6, to let a sense of urgency centered around a TBO grow and grow among managers and employees. Handle these tasks well, and all that follows is possible—even in an organization where a reasonable first reaction to the material in this book is "Not possible here."

EIGHT

GETTING STARTED

Q&A

We've been living in a world of single-system, hierar-chical organizations for so long that when a different form is proposed—even one as organic and intuitive as a dual system, even one already based on early success stories—it raises many questions. This is only natural. And while the basic idea of a dual system is simple, it can be challenging to implement depending on how deeply entrenched and exclusive the hierarchy is.

I and my colleagues have found that leaders who introduce the ideas in this book to their peers, key sub-ordinates, or bosses often encounter the same kinds of questions. How well they answer these questions can make the difference between moving ahead with a high probability of success or proceeding in a way that almost guarantees they will face unnecessary or debilitating problems later on.

Here are some of those common questions along with answers we have found to be helpful.

QUESTION: We already use something like this sort of structure in the form of interdepartmental task forces, "tiger teams," "self-managed work teams," or the like. This is basically the same, right?

ANSWER: These kinds of teams and task forces have some characteristics in common with a dual operating system, but overall the two are very different. Interdepartmental task forces and the like are controlled by, and work within, a single-system hierarchy. They are meant to supplement the twentieth-century organizational form to help it develop and execute new strategic and other initiatives in today's environment. The people who do the work on these teams are appointed (although sometimes the word "volunteer" is used, the reality is more like "volun-*told*"). Often they are directed by a project or program manager who is also appointed. Such teams rarely involve more than a few dozen people. They almost always go away after a set period of time. They usually use standard management processes: creating plans and measurements, defining accountability, setting timelines, reporting progress on all plans and milestones regularly to those higher up in the hierarchy.

Under the right circumstances, these vehicles can be very useful. But in terms of the sheer energy and alignment needed to help you stay ahead of fierce competition in a turbulent world, there is no comparison between them and a dual system.

QUESTION: We already know how to execute new strategies and have done so many times. Why would we want to move away from methods that have worked in the past and that people are comfortable with?

ANSWER: It is quite possible you *don't* have to move away from what you can do well. The issue is that what you have been doing probably needs some turbochargers, and for at least four big reasons.

First, consider how the world is changing, and therefore how we need to adjust to continue to win. The data are clear that events are accelerating, due mostly to technological breakthroughs and global integration. We are passing the point at which the old methods can continue to do the job effectively. As the saying goes, "What got you here won't get you there." Even for large-scale episodic change, there is very convincing evidence that organizations are now failing at least 70% of the time and that success in achieving early aspirations comes in fewer than 5% of cases. This fact is not widely known because people are reluctant to admit or advertise failures, for obvious reasons. And, to repeat: the successes in fewer than 5% of cases tend to be instances of very successful *episodic* change, not an ongoing series of strategic adjustments executed quickly in a tumultuous environment. The capability to do the latter can obviously be a huge strategic advantage.

Second, consider the stakes. The cautionary tale in chapter 3 tells us much. Handling strategic challenges poorly has always had serious consequences. For a large firm, the difference between success and failure has for decades potentially been billions in market capitalization. But today the difference is increasingly success versus total collapse.

Third, consider the risks. We normally shy away from anything that appears dramatically new because of the unknowns. Yet enterprises are being forced into critical reorganizations, major IT overhauls, or investments in emerging markets which have significantly greater risks than launching a dual system. The latter is an organic process and rarely requires any significant up-front investment.

Fourth, consider the comparison between your most recent successes and some of the early data we have on the results of dual systems: a doubling of revenue in just two years; a near doubling of market cap within thirty months; moving from a facility that was to be closed down to a model organization within its sector; transforming from a facility that was totally stuck in the past to one that is creating the future, and doing so in less than three years.

QUESTION: How can we measure the results of a dual system, or the network part of the system?

ANSWER: The GCs I have observed do try to measure results, but not in the way a management-driven hierarchy does. Left-side systems create measures relative to an operating plan. Accelerator networks don't have traditional operating plans. They have Big Opportunity statements, change visions, and a list of the current strategic initiatives and sub-initiatives. Left-side systems tend to ignore measurements that cannot be quantified. Accelerator networks measure the successes of initiatives quantitatively, but also with observations and inferences. Management-driven measurement systems tend to be created and monitored by sub-silos whose job it is to do just that. Right-side networks will allow initiative teams to create and use their own measures. So, there are many differences in measurement methods—all of which reflect the nature of innovative, fast, and agile start-ups versus that of mature, reliable, and efficient enterprises.

Some initiatives on the network side will produce results that can be easily calculated economically. A right-side initiative puts a new process in place that cuts purchasing costs by $X a year. A set of initiatives launch a new product in six months as opposed to the traditional nine months and at no extra cost. The incremental revenue during that three-month period adds $Y to this year's sales.

Some initiatives lead to valuable results that are observable, but harder to measure—for example: behavior changes that you have been trying to create for years, at who knows what cost, but without success. We saw one case in which top management had believed for a decade that better collaboration among sales teams from different product divisions would help increase revenues. Then the volunteer energy created by a right-side initiative led to what appeared to be true collaboration for the first time ever! Or you have wanted greater employee engagement, and the new system seems to create it. Or you have been trying, unsuccessfully, to create a culture of innovation, and with the new dual system it seems to be happening.

Some right-side measures will be quantitative but indirect in the sense that one cannot totally prove a causal relationship. These are often leading indicators. For example: A dual system as a whole may have contributed to a feeling among employees, measured on yearly attitude surveys, that a firm is a better place to work, and that, some people think, is why they are getting Z% more people applying for jobs. Or performance appraisal forms show a measurable uptick in the number of people receiving better ratings for "leadership," and those people more often than not have played some role in the networked system. Or—maybe impossible to measure with any accuracy, yet indicative of what the network is doing—people simply feel more energy in the offices or plants, energy sparked by the most active participants in the new dual system.

QUESTION: How do I hold people in the network accountable for the work they commit to do? What metrics do I use to measure individual performance? What compensation structure succeeds best in rewarding people for their right-side work?

ANSWER: These are logical left-side questions. They must be sorted out clearly in any management-driven hierarchy or that system simply cannot do its job well. But things like accountability, metrics, and compensation for individuals are not the essential material of a strategy-accelerator network. In a right-side organization, it is urgency, passion, open communication, empowerment, a "want to" operating principle, and leadership from many that are the central issues at the core of success—and the Accelerators, as described in this book, directly deal with these issues.

That does not mean that no one pays attention to accountability in a well-functioning right-side organization. But because of the very different nature of the system, people hold each other accountable for playing their roles. Since metrics are helpful in keeping track of progress on initiatives or in identifying wins that should be celebrated, teams create their own metrics. I have yet to see a case in which a compensation scheme is required to make a right-side network work. People participate for reasons other than compensation.

QUESTION: Who does a right-side network report to?

ANSWER: Again, "report to" is not really the most apt concept for describing the relationship between the two parts of a dual system. It is, and must be, a symbiotic partnership. It is true that for the system to work and sustain itself, the left-side executive committee must choose to set the network up, allow it to function, and role model supportive behavior. Because the left side is where the official structure and governance reside, it will have great influence on the network and has the authority to shut it down at any time. It also must either generate or buy into the Big Opportunity, which acts as a North Star and primary motivator for the network.

But from the beginning, the GC and the executive committee must develop a close partnership to help keep the two sides well connected, working as one organization, and strategically aligned but not working on the same tasks in ways that waste resources. It does take some time and effort to create the best sort of partnership—but I have seen people do it and, as a result, greatly contribute to outstanding performance by their firms.

QUESTION: Then who runs the right side? The guiding coalition? If yes, who runs the GC? And how?

ANSWER: It's not really a question of "running" the right side. "Guide" or "lead" are more accurate words than "run," and the core group (the GC) does that. In successful dual systems, the GC has many functions, including (1) making sure the network has a change vision that is totally aligned with the Big Opportunity; (2) agreeing on what the primary strategic initiatives are at any one point in time and making sure they are aligned with the change vision as well as any left-side strategic plans and strategic initiatives; (3) keeping in tight communication with the executive committee, but not as in a left-side reporting relationship; (4) monitoring, but not controlling, what is happening in the strategy-accelerator network, looking out for unnoticed overlap between initiatives on the right and left, and facilitating communication and problem solving among initiatives; (5) looking for and celebrating wins; and (6) in general keeping the accelerator processes working well.

As for who runs the GC: no one does in a hierarchical sense. A facilitator helps it to work as a team. There are always one or two "go-to" people who emerge (organically) and help lead each major initiative. There may be a few people in the GC who emerge as particularly strong leaders to whom others look when there are disagreements or confusion. But there is no traditional formal hierarchy.

QUESTION: How much time and effort will be needed from senior leaders and other managers to put this new system into place?

ANSWER: Because the new system is organic to the organization—not a separate gigantic project that needs to be designed, evaluated, resourced, and managed, and not a huge reorganization that must be planned and executed—the answer is remarkably little. What senior leaders do, or do not do, in buying into, supporting, and helping guide the development of a dual system is exceptionally important. But the time demands are very modest, except possibly for those who personally volunteer to work in the right-side system. For all the rest of higher-level management, their right-side activities—including launching the process with a Big Opportunity exercise, learning the principles and processes and structure, keeping connected to the GC in an appropriate partnership, and demonstrating enthusiasm for right-side successes—might require 5% of their time, but no more. That means, on average, about two hours a week. It is a very important two hours, and for some it will be a challenging two hours because the process is so different and new for them. But a time demand that cuts into normal left-side activities and commitments? No.

Much more than time, the issue here is behavior within the small slice of time. It is all about leadership, not management. It is about role modeling what the hierarchy needs to do to allow the network to grow. So much of this is simple: broadcasting the Big Opportunity statement. Patting people on the back when they create a win.

And for the head of the unit creating a dual system, this is obviously particularly important. He or she can't appoint someone else to be the head of the new "project." Strategic acceleration and dual systems are not a project. The boss must see the value and show it.

QUESTION: Obviously, outsourcing the building of a dual system to masses of smart, report-writing, deliverables-providing management consultants has no chance of working. But our people and management are already stretched. How can we possibly make this happen?

ANSWER: The point about outsourcing is correct. And yes, so many people inside organizations are feeling stretched. But the whole Accelerator process is designed, and has many times proven itself able, to get much more output from the same input.

The very first Accelerator step, done well, leaves large groups of people with a sense of urgency, and energy, around a Big Opportunity—an opportunity that seems to them both sensible and emotionally compelling. This makes all the difference in the world in drawing people to be volunteers, doing their regular jobs plus more, and keeping them from dropping out due to normal left-side pressures.

True urgency around an emotionally appealing opportunity taps into people's genuine desire to do something meaningful. It taps into the passions that are in all of us but so often have little chance for expression on the job. It connects with sources of energy within people who really want their organizations to win and who are appalled when missions are not accomplished, competitors are not beaten, or customers are not served exceptionally well. The Accelerators are designed and intended to tap into this energy and keep tapping into it—and to afford those in the network the thrill of winning, of camaraderie with people they normally would never meet, and of personal growth. When this happens, you will find that people's bandwidth suddenly expands dramatically.

The key issue here is that people's energy levels are not a zero-sum number. It's not the case that, if 20% of your capacity goes into network activities, there is only 80% left over for your regular job. People can expand their energy and expertise to 120% or 150% of current levels, and in a well-functioning dual system they do. If you have never seen this, it can, quite logically, be hard to believe. But most of us *have seen* this, at least within the context of a whole life. Think of the parent who has no spare time but somehow makes time, without shirking other commitments, when his or her child needs tutoring to do well in school. Or the man who is "exhausted" at the end of the workday yet is building a twenty-five-foot boat in his backyard with energy that comes from . . . where?

And one of the additional benefits of involvement in a strategy-accelerator network is that people come to appreciate and distinguish better between what is truly important to success in a fast-moving, turbulent world and what are merely low-value-added activities left over from the past. They can use this knowledge to re-prioritize work in their regular jobs and drop irrelevant yet time-consuming activities—freeing up bandwidth for what is truly important to them.

QUESTION: How do I keep enthusiastic volunteers from shirking their regular jobs?

ANSWER: A well-run hierarchy does not allow this. The whole system of bosses, measurements, perfor-mance appraisal, and accountability catches and corrects shirking.

Also, in a well-run dual system, people who work on both sides understand that left-side shirking is not acceptable and that if they must drop out of a right-side initiative for a while to deal with immediate left-side pressures, that is fine. One beauty of fast and agile networks is that when someone drops out, others fill the gap immediately. No time is needed to post a job opening, interview candidates, select one, negotiate salary, or anything else. In this sense, the network side of a dual system is much more akin to a fire brigade, lined up and passing pails of water from a well to the fire, than to replacing someone in a normal company or government bureau. One person leaves and the network of volunteers adjusts quickly.

QUESTION: How do I make sure volunteers keep their focus on strategically important issues and not low-priority pet projects?

ANSWER: In building a dual system, the whole process is centered around a genuine opportunity that is sensible, aligned with an existing company strategy, and exciting for people to contemplate. A properly crafted Big Opportunity statement alone provides guardrails on right-side work and will keep out many a pet project.

Moreover, because a right-side network is not hierarchical, if someone tries to launch a sub-initiative which is not the least bit strategically relevant, some people will flag the issue (usually because they are not worried about repercussions from bosses for speaking up, since there are no right-side bosses).

And, in an effective dual system, the right side's change vision and strategic initiatives are aligned with a Big Opportunity statement and ultimately agreed upon by both the GC and the executive committee—more guardrails.

QUESTION: How do you keep the two sides together? Even more important, how do you keep their actions well aligned?

ANSWER: Education helps. You tell them what we know today about dual systems and the roles of top management and a GC. The fact that the people in the network have jobs in the hierarchy helps. And continuous, engaged communication is key—between the GC and the executive committee as well as between volunteers when they are back in their regular jobs on the left side and all of their fellow employees.

In terms of coordination, we have found that the most important rule of thumb is this: before you start on a new activity, check to make sure that the work you wish to focus on is not already being done well on the left side.

A challenging issue arises when initiatives are already being done on the left side but poorly, and the people involved do not see the problem and most certainly don't want help in solving what they view as a non-problem. This could be in any area: a project that is examining the firm's performance appraisal or bonus system, a program to launch a communication campaign on a new product, a task force evaluating the next generation of heavy machinery used in a plant. In a well-functioning dual system, the people on the right learn that lecturing people on the left about their flawed approaches will usually create only conflict, wasted time, and stresses. Here again is where the correct processes come into play. The right side sees this problem as simply another barrier to needed change—a normal part of life in all organizations—and one of the Accelerators mobilizes and directs the creativity, passion, and energy on the right side to find a practical way to knock down the barrier.

QUESTION: Should all strategic initiatives be handled by the right-side network?

ANSWER: No. Here's a general rule for determining what goes where. All processes and activities that do not require change, or that involve doing what we know how to do, stay on the left side. Thus any strategic changes that are unambiguous—where we know exactly where we need to go (from A to B) and the distance is not far, where there won't be huge resistance from people, where innovation is not a big issue, where we know how to achieve the goal within the time frame of the window of opportunity—these usually go on the left side. They will be driven by strategic planning organizations, project management organizations, traditional task forces, change management departments, and the like.

On the other hand, high-stakes initiatives that will likely involve a lot of change, where speed is important, where there are ambiguities, or where innovation and agility will be needed, go on the right side. In an increasingly fast-moving world, the number of such initiatives is increasing all the time.

Another way to think of this: any strategic activity, innovative activity, or change-related activity that we know can be effectively completed in a timely way and at acceptable expense inside a management hierarchy framework usually stays there. So if we consider an initiative, done every four years, to look at some part of the employee benefits package, and if the level of complaints about the package is low and no new legislation has added additional problems or opportunities, then the project should stay left.

In general, if the left side can do a job, but more speed, less expense, or more creativity would be very helpful, then a right-side organization might help with its volunteers. If, for example, due to new legislation the benefits project suddenly has to be completed in three months instead of six, then the right might become involved in helping the left to accelerate activity.

If, for all practical purposes, the left side cannot do the job at all—might not even see that a job is needed, much less be able to complete it before a window of opportunity slams shut or its budget is destroyed—then the initiative goes right.

QUESTION: What sort of budget does the network side need, and who sets the budget?

ANSWER: A right-side organization does not have a budget per se. All financial resources are controlled by the management hierarchy because the left side is ultimately held accountable for financial success by a board of directors. It is the job of the GC and all the volunteers to find resources, when they need them, and to convince people on the left to allocate money for specific initiatives. A right-side initiative which cannot find any resources on the left—even with energetic people making the case again and again, even with GC members and other volunteers being creative about whom to approach, and how and when—almost always is a bad idea, a flawed solution to a problem, or a solution for which no problem or opportunity in fact exists. Therefore the idea should not be pursued, for the good of the organization.

Practically, this works out just fine, because the right side is always a convince-me, lead-me organization, not a do-what-I-say, manage-me organization. The fact that an accelerator network has no budget, and must rely on the left, also has the practical benefit of being just one more way of keeping the two sides connected and working as one system, not two.

QUESTION: How do you keep people from doing what they know, going back to hierarchical behaviors, when they are doing network work?

ANSWER: We call this "the default problem."

More specifically, the default problem occurs when people, usually under stress, revert to what they know: left-side processes, principles, methods, and techniques. And they can revert in the blink of an eye.

So instead of always relying on volunteers to help with establishing a sense of urgency among many employees around a big strategic opportunity, we'll sometimes see leaders suddenly fall back to appointing (often very busy) people to do the job. Instead of allowing passionate volunteers to work on strategic initiatives, someone suddenly starts to appoint people (often those "with the right skill sets"). Instead of right-side groups working on what they have the most energy and passion for, they suddenly focus on what they think they should focus on. Instead of a GC organizing itself as the core of a network, it starts to turn itself into a hierarchy. And you start to project manage an initiative team. You turn over communication activities to where (you think) they belong: the communications department. Leaders stop thinking in terms of many change agents and start involving fewer and fewer people. The right side shrinks into more of an idea-generating mechanism (at best they "think outside the box") instead of an idea-generating and -implementing group ("working outside the box"). Wins—so essential in helping a network to gain confidence, build credibility, and grow—are ignored unless they fit the hierarchy's measurement systems. And any of this can happen in a flash, even right in the middle of a meeting.

The best solution to the default problem is vigilance. Everyone involved—every single volunteer—watches for defaults. The senior leadership looks for defaults. When people see the problem, they wave a flag and help move action back in the right direction.

QUESTION: What is the single biggest challenge in creating a dual system?

ANSWER: Getting started, and in the right way. And the right way is what I have outlined in the previous two chapters.

NINE

THE (INEVITABLE)
FUTURE OF STRATEGY

Predicting the future is a perilous activity. But if you look at enough data, you can see there are some trends pointing in a pretty clear direction.

EXPONENTIAL CHANGE

Consider, once again, the graphs at the start of chapter 1. These show not only increasing change in a number of arenas but also an exponential trend in the amount of change. More is coming at us faster. One can logically make an argument that the trend lines in these graphs will flatten out or go into a downward slope at some point soon. But the argument that a flattening or downward trend will continue for any significant time, before the numbers flash upward again, is not a very convincing one.

In fact, it is very difficult to look at data and evidence from the field and come to any other conclusion than that our world will continue to accelerate, quite possibly at an increased rate. If this is true, then it is very difficult to believe that the twentieth-century organization, amazing machine though it may be, can succeed in handling a world moving so much faster and more unpredictably. If we don't shift to a new way of operating, the consequences will be severe—for businesses, governments, economies, societies, and, ultimately, for the many billions of people living on our planet.

On the other hand, if we can successfully implement a new way of running organizations that not only can handle this new environment but actually takes advantage of it, the possibilities for making better products and services, enlarging wealth, and creating more and better jobs may be hard to comprehend. An increasingly changing world does have potentially serious downside consequences. But there is also a potentially huge upside.

THE EVOLUTION OF STRATEGY

An important implication of the dual operating system described in this book, and the context to which it is responding, is that we need a whole new notion of "strategy."

"Strategy" is a term used loosely to mean high-level policies designed to help you successfully achieve your most important goals, or, in a competitive context, to help you win. As a modern concept of relevance to organizations, strategy is a relatively new idea. When I began my career, it was not even a term used at Harvard Business School, much less a required course in the MBA curriculum there (or anywhere). Executives in businesses did not talk of "strategic planning" or "strategic thinking." Of course, all mature organizations *had* strategies, often developed many years earlier, when they were young. But the strategies were implicit. They were simply taken as a given—frameworks which shaped and constrained the context in which firms did their yearly operational planning.

Then, between 1965 and 1975, that all changed as the nature of competition began to change.

Among companies, this was largely because of the Japanese, whose exports in autos and consumer electronics disrupted relatively stable competition in the developed world, especially the United States. Wider availability of powerful computing capability suddenly allowed firms to gather and analyze data on costs and market share, and for the first time gave them clearer insight into their real competitive situations, assets, and vulnerabilities.

Economic competition among nations began to change, particularly because of OPEC. Rather suddenly, some petroleum-exporting nations had significant competitive leverage over other countries.

In a parallel world, there was a small revolution in thinking about competition. In the 1960s, business historian Alfred Chandler, then teaching at MIT's Sloan School of Management, wrote an influential book with the title *Strategy and Structure*. Bruce Henderson began the first modern strategy consulting practice, building it into the Boston Consulting Group. In the 1970s, Michael Porter created a course at Harvard called "Competitive Strategy" and then published a book with that title.

By the 1980s, guided in part by the intellectual leadership of Porter and Henderson and those that followed them, "strategic planning" departments were added to more and more businesses. The track record for effectiveness varied greatly. But in some cases, this entirely new aspect of management was wildly successful. Jack Welch's strategic dictum that General Electric would operate only in markets where it could be number 1 or number 2 helped transform the firm and produced hugely increased economic performance. Other business leaders noticed and began seeking good strategic ideas and developing their own.

The strategic consulting industry grew from nothing to tens of billions of dollars in yearly revenues. Both Bruce Henderson and his intellectual offspring, Bill Bain, built incredibly successful global enterprises that had not even existed in 1960. McKinsey, the grande dame of management consulting, caught on late but then came on strong. McKinsey may have had less than a hundred employees in 1950. Today it has tens of thousands.

The strategic sophistication of the typical firm today is vastly superior to what it was in 1970. Today it is hard to find a business that does not talk in terms of strategy. Increasingly, the same is true for nonprofit organizations, government agencies, and even universities.

Today strategy is thought of as having two basic components: creation and implementation. The first is implicitly treated as by far the most important. The process is linear: create strategy, then implement strategy. Typically enterprises do strategic planning once a year, as a part of their operational planning exercise. The "best practice" methods used to do that planning, and the implementation of the plans, are some variation of what I very briefly described in chapter 4 and will elaborate in appendix A. The methods work hand-in-glove with a management-driven hierarchy. The key players in making strategic decisions, and directing the implementation, always sit at the top of the hierarchy.

As the world moves faster and faster, and more firms create dual operating systems, it is hard to believe that this pattern won't be forced to change significantly. Strategy won't operate only on a yearly cycle because opportunities and hazards don't operate on a yearly cycle. Creation and implementation will start to blur as new data are discovered during implementation which immediately need to inform new creation.

This is already happening. Today, strategy is being viewed in some organizations more as a dynamic force, not one directed by a strategic planning department and put into a yearly planning cycle. It is a force that constantly seeks opportunities, identifies initiatives to capitalize on them, and completes those initiatives swiftly and efficiently. I think of that force as an ongoing process of searching, doing, learning, and modifying. Among mature organizations, you find this most often in the dual system described in this book. The Accelerator processes driving the network serve as a continuous, holistic, and innovative strategic change function, one that quickens momentum and agility because it never stops. This imparts a kind of strategic "fitness" to the organization—the more it exercises its strategy skills, the more adept it becomes at dealing with a hypercompetitive environment and the more those skills become a part of its DNA or culture.

Number crunching will continue to be important, but in a rapidly changing and turbulent world numerical data become more fluid and ambiguous. More eyes and ears and hearts need to be in the strategy game, not just a limited number of senior managers. And that is what a dual system can do.

I suppose it may be hard for people who have lived their professional lives in mature organizations to imagine this radical change in how we think about and handle strategy. It will be much less difficult for successful entrepreneurs and the young.

THE DUAL SYSTEM . . . AND YOU

We still have many details to work out, in terms of how this new form of organization and concept of strategy will function. But some pioneers—such as those described in this book—have already shown that these approaches work in the real world. Dual systems, which can handle strategy in a very different way than is the norm today, are helping people to thrive and win.

With all the challenges we face, it is easy to make a pessimistic argument about the era in which we live and work, and about the future. I will not make that argument here. I believe the optimistic scenario is far stronger. I know there are some very capable and intelligent people who would disagree with me. But as I write this, I have no hesitations in my judgments.

So let's get on with the job.

APPENDIX A

CAN YOUR
"BEST PRACTICES" SAVE YOU?
An Assessment

In chapter 4 I explained how, in order to cope with a faster-moving and more turbulent world, organizations everywhere use some combination of three "best practice" approaches to enhance the capabilities of systems not designed for speed and agility. The question here is: which of these methods do you use and, given the information in this appendix, what is a reasonable assessment of how well those approaches are going to work for you today and in the future?

Approach #1: Stretch Operational Planning and Execution to Include Strategic Components

In this first option, a firm adds strategic planning into its yearly operational planning process in an effort to identify strategic challenges earlier and create new strategic initiatives in a more timely manner. It also then executes any funded initiatives through the hierarchy in the same manner it executes a quarterly plan.

Functional groups, area units, or product divisions do additional number gathering and analysis. They may even write business cases for any new strategic initiatives which explain and justify the funds needed to support the work. The cases then go to the executive committee, which examines them as a part of its regular yearly planning process and approves or does not approve the strategic choices, the strategic initiatives, and the funding requests.

Any approved new initiatives, along with their budgets, are then executed through the hierarchy in the same way that any operational plan, and its associated budget, is executed. So the marketing department, the European division, or the consumer appliances product division simply expands plans to include both regular operational activities as well as these new strategic activities. The monthly budgets will reflect this. The agendas in regular management meetings will reflect this. New metrics may be added to follow the strategic parts of the plan, but these will be only an extension of, not a shift in, the regular measurement systems. In conjunction with traditional compensation, new incentives may be added for successfully meeting the metrics set for the strategic parts of the plan. But the compensation system will not change in any fundamental way. For all practical purposes, nothing changes except that what is being managed expands to a longer time frame. There may be no economic payoff this quarter or even this year. In fact, the opposite is usually true, because initiatives drain cash and so reduce quarterly reported profits.

The consequences: In some cases this method can work just fine. The resources need to be available to invest in initiatives which have no immediate payoff. When the external changes, the ambiguities, and the competitive pressures are not so great, the new strategy or initiatives will not need to be big, or much different from what you have been doing, and the existing methodology for running the enterprise can handle that well. With strategic initiatives that are smaller in scope, the corresponding resistance that emerges to these changes is rarely that significant. Again, approach #1 can handle that too. If there are any problems, a strong CEO can simply apply more pressure to get the strategic part as well as the operational part of a plan done. Sometimes, with just that additional commitment and pressure from the top, this method succeeds.

Basically, the hierarchy and management systems force change to happen, and that works when the change is not large in scale. Occasionally the head of the organization and the communications department may need to use normal communication channels and methods to cascade a special message down the hierarchy to create buy-in and so reduce annoying resistance. But normal is the operative word. Nothing fundamentally new is needed with this approach except that you stretch the time frame in planning and executing.

Increasingly, however, this method is no longer a winning formula. A management-driven hierarchical system was invented for efficiency, reliability, and constancy. With sound structure and competent people, it can be a marvel at doing work at minimum cost and at the quality expected, and doing both each and every day, week after week, month after month. Yes, its processes can be stretched a bit to include initiatives that may slightly change the nature of the work that is done. But after a while, you run into four problems.

First, a management-driven hierarchical system is very much designed to focus on the *now*. This is one of the criticisms people have been leveling at it for some thirty years. It has an exceptionally strong bias for the short term: the day, the week, the quarter. You can add into its planning and control processes initiatives that have longer time frames, but when pressure is put on the system it defaults to its short-term design in a nanosecond.

We have all seen this. The agenda for the executive committee meeting may allow thirty minutes for operational issues and thirty minutes for strategic issues. But when problems arise—and they always do, even more so in a faster-moving and more unpredictable world—what wins out in the meetings? Managers have been endlessly criticized in the past few decades for letting the 30-30 agenda slide to 55-5. But what the critics often miss is that this problem is inherent in the *system*. It has nothing to do with shortsighted or incompetent managers.

Second, a well-designed structure has what we derisively call "silos" for a reason: to create focused attention and expertise in order to make work less expensive, more reliable, and more dependable. The goal is to minimize, for example, the cost and time needed for important communication by grouping critical communication links inside silos. But when you start to add strategic initiatives that try to do work differently to meet new demands, it is exceptionally rare that all the needed change will be limited to only one silo or sub-silo. Organizations are filled with interdependencies, as when changes in new product development demand a new product launch process, which in turn requires changes in marketing and sales. So more communication across silos is inevitably needed. And, in a hierarchy, if the volume of change goes beyond a fairly low level, that communication does not happen effectively.

In addition, any new working arrangements may demand shifting resources from one silo or sub-silo to another. The average human being does not like to give up resources and promotion opportunities. So people resist. Resistance slows action and costs money.

Third, all hierarchies have levels, again to ensure efficiencies and reliability. People in very narrow and specialized jobs at the bottom can become very good at doing their work without mistakes and without requiring high salaries. In a world that does not change much, the people at the top have all the information they need to make good strategic decisions, and the people at the bottom have all the information they need to implement those decisions. But with more speed and uncertainty, neither group automatically has the facts it needs, so more information must go up and down the hierarchy more frequently—and it must be valid. This does not happen easily. Information moves slowly up and down levels, and all sorts of factors distort its validity.

Fourth, the odds of putting together a strategic plan which makes accurate predictions for two years, much less five or more, start to decrease as the world speeds up and becomes more unpredictable. So the plans, which are already hard to execute, are also now not very good. But with a once-a-year planning cycle, you have very limited ability to change plans as reality changes around you. The needed agility and speed are not there. Windows of opportunity open and then close before you see them, much less go through them. Torpedoes hit your ship before you are able to accelerate out of the way. And struggling with all these problems can even detract from your ability to meet your short-term commitments. Not a winning formula.

I have seen dozens and dozens of cases with these problems in the past decade. In most, the end result is not disastrous—when people see their methods are not working, they simply search for new solutions and move on to one or both of the approaches I describe below. But they always pay some cost. A consumer products company's market position slips from number 2 to number 3. A military contractor loses a big contract and sees its revenue growth go flat. A manufacturing function cannot reinvent itself fast enough to improve productivity, and the firm's profits drop even as revenues continue to increase.

Approach #2: Augment Your Basic System with New Units (Permanent or Temporary), People, and Reporting Relationships

The next solution organizations use to stay competitive in a faster-changing world is to augment the hierarchy with new units, people, and relationships, usually added one at a time.

In this case, you try to deal with the huge bias to the short term by creating units with no basic operational responsibilities: strategic planning departments, strategy consultants, project management offices only for strategic initiatives. You add new units that focus specifically on change issues: a change management group. You staff the units with new specialists: people in the strategic planning office or the strategy consultants have analytical abilities to deal with more uncertain contexts. You add task forces and workstreams and tiger teams with people from multiple silos to try to deal with the silo communication and coordination problems.

To a point, this solution also helps. Agility and speed increase. But after a while, you run into the same four problems encountered with the first approach: the default back to the short term; silo communication and coordination problems (which are now multiplied because with the new units, you have created new short-term and long-term silos); the inherent limitations in how fast and accurately information will go up and down hierarchies; and dealing with too much uncertainty when trying to develop new strategies.

You also add another big problem: cost. All the new people require additional funds, which can make it difficult (or impossible) to hit the short-term economic targets demanded by the capital markets. You could spread the addition of the new people out over time, but that would slow everything down. And there is a secondary cost consideration: an augmented staff has a tendency to find new needs. Smart people can always find new reasons for needing bigger budgets.

This second approach can sometimes also fail because executives find themselves going back to the same people again and again to head task forces, be sponsors, or take on new roles. Great people, no matter how charismatic or energetic, wear out. So what do you do? Augment more by bringing in superstars from the outside (which takes time and is expensive)? Cut back on the number of initiatives (which, if they are really needed, slows you down and means you miss opportunities)? It can feel like a vicious cycle.

I run into this all the time. Again, the results are often not catastrophic, but they lead to a slow decline. You may find executives frustrated at the organization's inability to respond rapidly to opportunities, but whose attempts to solve the problem are not very successful. And excuses are always available. We are in an increasingly regulated industry. Our present speed is all that is possible. The staff entrusted with compliance constantly put up stop signs. It's frustrating but perhaps inevitable. We are so big that bureaucracy seems all around us. Slowness is natural. The pushback we are encountering is just human nature. What can you do?

Often, the slow movement and the problems causing it are not very visible at the top of the hierarchy, which can lead to a deceptive or even dangerous situation. The new program management office makes regular reports on the progress of the execution of strategic initiatives, and all of these show that you are close to being on time. And those reports continue in just that way until something blows up. A major customer abandons you because a competitor comes out with the next generation of your leading product line earlier than you had anticipated and well before your new product development and sales strategy has been executed. Or all is reported to be fine until the program managers themselves are suddenly given data that unforeseen problems will cause major delays.

Approach #3: Use Acquisitions to Speed Up

The whole idea with this approach is not to take the time to invent the next generation of your product or service; not to take the time to develop strong customer loyalty in your fastest-growing market segment; not to take the time to innovate here, there, and everywhere; not to build agility and speed—but just to buy it.

With this method, you usually hire M&A specialists, strategic consultants, or both to help you. You pay for the advice, and you pay for the acquisition. This often leads to a series of small acquisitions, which you then try to consolidate and build on. Under very specific circumstances, this method can be effective. You have to be able to afford the acquisitions. The people in the acquired enterprises must, to some minimum degree, not hate the idea of being bought. The differences in cultures between your organization and those you have acquired cannot be too large. But if the conditions are just right, an organization can use acquisitions to accelerate and be more successful—at least for a while.

But increasingly, there are more problems with this approach than there are solutions. In a faster-moving and more ambiguous world, the M&A specialists and the strategic consultants are not necessarily equipped to pick the best candidates for acquisition. The acquisitions can, of course, be expensive. The people making or selling your current products or services may not like abandoning what they know and taking on the next generation of products or services as invented by someone else. Transferring customer loyalty in high-growth segments from the acquired to the acquirer will almost always turn out to be complex (and dealing with the complexities takes time). And acquirers that are big management-driven hierarchies have a remarkable ability to smash those great toys they just spent a lot of money on.

Almost no one seems to know the true track record for these sorts of acquisitions. People who fail have no incentive to make the facts public. The M&A world includes some very smart people who have a huge vested interest in convincing us that their acquisitions succeed. In general, the studies of this approach done by neutral third parties, typically academics, show disappointing results. Acquisition negotiations fall apart for all sorts of reasons. Acquisition targets fight back. You succeed with the transaction but pay too much. You succeed with the transaction but never integrate cultures to the degree needed to support the projected business strategy. Or the newly acquired entities fight fiercely to keep their autonomy and all the fighting distracts attention from meeting both short-term numbers and longer-term strategic challenges.

The fundamental problem here, as with the other options described in this appendix, is the same: they all still work within the framework of a single-system, management-driven hierarchy. All these best practices modify or add small or large elements onto that hierarchy. Done well, all can add some agility or speed. But ultimately, yours is still an organization designed for efficiency, reliability, and consistency and not even remotely designed for innovation, bold strategy creation and execution, and most of all agility and speed. Acquisitions, strategy committees, mega–interdepartmental task forces, and new metrics focusing on the strategic parts of a plan are like fancy (and sometimes expensive) new baubles or lights or streamers put on a holiday tree. Each addition can make the tree prettier. Some are more dramatic in what they do than others. But in the end, you still have a holiday tree—which most certainly is not a creation built to race around the living room.

Successful organizations will try to venture down still other paths, but they are rarer. Sometimes an enterprise will react to failures with the "ornaments method" by madly doing more and more of the same—adding a quality program, a joint venture, a full-blown merger—until the result is just the opposite of the intention. The entity becomes more bloated and less agile. Everything slows down even more. Energy is drained out of the system as change fatigue spreads everywhere. The costs of the ornaments kill quarterly profits or blow up budgets.

So—does any of this look familiar? Is your organization depending on one or more of these approaches? If yes, and it seems to be working for now, how long can that last? Are your "best practices" really going to save you?

APPENDIX B

DO YOU NEED TO TAKE ACTION NOW?

An Assessment

A simple but profoundly important question is: do you need to be developing a fully functioning dual operating system *now*? Not next year or sometime in the future, but now?

In light of the stakes involved, have you crossed the line where traditional methods can no longer guarantee that you will be able to develop and implement new strategies and strategic initiatives in ways that are innovative, agile, and quick enough to stay up with or keep ahead of competitors?

That line can be murky, but you can make an informed assessment about where you are by asking and answering a set of questions. Precision in doing so is impossible. But that is not the biggest problem here. The problem is that far too often, for all sorts of reasons, most associated with the very nature of management-driven hierarchies, too few of the right issues are explicitly raised in the first place. People assume they know the answers without serious information gathering and analysis. Too little time is explicitly spent in a serious discussion of the issues.

The Magnitude of Relevant External Change

The most basic question here is: what strategic challenges do you have because of what is changing around you, might soon change, has recently changed, or is changing faster in a way that will significantly affect your business? This would include change related to competitors, technology, suppliers, customers, government demands, your workforce demographics, product life cycles, and so on.

More specifically: because of what is happening in the marketplace, do you need to take your organization up an entire level in its capabilities to continue to grow profitably?

Are traditional competitors making bold moves that put you at risk? Are new competitors from India or China, for example, poised to take away a significant part of your business?

Has there been an extended period of time since your organization last went through a significant change, such that the gap between what is required by your environment and what you can do has grown sufficiently that you need to accelerate ASAP?

Has anything changed recently that opens a new and big window of opportunity to win new customers, increase market capitalization, grow profitably, or offer revolutionary products?

These are hardly mysterious questions, but the very nature of running a single-system organization often doesn't allow people enough time to reflect on them sufficiently. For almost everyone in a hierarchy, there is simply too much to do each week in dealing with the endless number of personnel, sales, purchasing, and financial issues that flood managerial calendars. Even when time is taken to access new opportunities or threats, the powerful inward focus of management processes and the inherent difficulty of pulling relevant data up hierarchical levels can make this task challenging. Often most of all, the silos inherent in management-driven hierarchies offer different answers to these questions, leaving executive committees nonaligned.

The Stakes

What are the true stakes involved in not dealing well with your strategic challenges?

If market share does dip, or is dipping, can that lead to the sort of consequences seen in the case in chapter 3?

Could you slip from number 1 to number 2 in your businesses . . . or from number 5 to number 6? Could you be sliced and diced out of existence?

Is a technological discontinuity possible that could have disastrous consequences?

Could you be left as a small enough player in your industry that strong profits will become impossible?

What would happen to you strategically and economically if a competitor offered a better alternative for the next generation of your products, or offered it faster than you can?

And what are the true upside possibilities? What are the big opportunities offered if your organization were able to move swiftly and with agility?

All leaders pay some attention to these issues. But, as the case in chapter 3 shows, management-driven hierarchies lead people to underestimate the stakes in a world which presents more and more strategic challenges. And for perfectly understandable reasons, they lead the average person to *vastly* underestimate what is at stake.

The Magnitude of Internal Change Required

How many employees will need to change their behavior in some non-trivial way because of large external threats or opportunities?

Or how much change will be required from managers and staff because you have committed to execute a bold new strategy?

Without serious and open-minded reflection, it is easy to make this judgment inaccurately. People may say: "Seventy people in the IT department will need to change significantly what they do as a result of the successful execution of this strategic initiative." You ask: "But won't their actions mean that thousands of secretaries, professionals, and middle managers will be looking at a different desktop on their computers and be required to learn Arrfx, Duddol, or Praxix, which is not an easy task? And won't some of them be changing away from a system that they have been using for a decade? Aren't many of these people at remote locations? And how many really think this disruption in their routine is necessary?"

Or people may say: "Our innovation initiative means a hundred employees in product development will have to change how they create new offerings for the company." You ask: "But won't that lead to products which will then require new and different actions by almost the entire sales force? Won't it demand a new model, a new way of thinking, for at least the hundreds of people selling one key line of products?"

The problem here is associated with the complex interdependencies built into modern organizations. A is connected to B which is connected to C which in turn affects A. A map of all the relationships created by inter-dependencies often looks impossibly complex and confusing. In a stable world, all that doesn't matter much. B doesn't change, so its link to C is irrelevant. But how stable is your world?

Without serious attention to this question, it is not unusual to find that people think relatively complex, difficult, or significant changes may be needed from 10% of the employee population where 50% would be a better guess. When you are talking about a percentage of the employee population that really is in the single digits or low double digits, when the changes needed are clear, and when the shifts can be made incrementally over three to five years, you often have a challenge that an enhanced management-driven hierarchy can handle easily. With more people, more ambiguity, and less time, it probably can't handle the challenge.

Your Recent Experiences with an Enhanced Hierarchy

Over the past year, if you have assigned people to a task force or committee to deal with significant strategic opportunities or threats, how have they behaved? How much time did they put into the work, and was that time sufficient?

If the strategy work was exported to a consulting firm, and their people interviewed your managers and employees, how did your people react? How many felt threatened or felt the exercise was a terrible waste of time and money? How did those people behave during and after the interviews?

If you appointed executives as "champions" or "sponsors" for the work of initiative teams, how much time did they spend on this role? If their peers felt inconvenienced or threatened by the change that a champion's group was trying to make, what did the champion do?

If the execution of a strategic change was put into a project management framework, how well did that approach handle subtle resistance from people who didn't understand the change, didn't see the need for the change, disagreed with it, or felt threatened by it?

How agile has your entire strategic process been in adjusting to shifting conditions? In creating the right new initiatives? In executing fast enough?

It is easy to identify another half-dozen questions of the same ilk. A C-suite is often given soothing answers in formal project or initiative review meetings—until serious problems, with serious consequences in terms of time and cost, become blatantly obvious.

Cultural Change

How likely is it that addressing the strategic issues you face will require some significant cultural change on the part of the organization?

Put another way: will successful execution of your strategic initiatives make you alter the way you have been operating for many years? Will it require that you change some fairly ingrained individual habits or group norms?

How has your strategy execution method dealt with this issue? What is your track record in making important cultural changes effectively and in a timely manner?

Strategic Changes That Are Already Underway

If you are using traditional methods (task forces, tiger teams, strategy consultants, and so forth)—or even those methods put on steroids—is the pace of success adequate?

Is the cost of this approach acceptable in light of short-term pressures?

Is continuing the use of these methods a sustainable approach for the foreseeable future?

If your answers are satisfying, consider these caveats. In dealing with a specific strategic challenge, a traditional system can produce what seems like adequate progress for a while. That is exactly what happened in the case in chapter 3. Or execution will seem to work, but when you are "done," activities and behaviors will begin to revert back to where they were before you began.

I have found this problem to be more common than you might think, and (obviously) very dangerous. The consequences go beyond one strategic failure. In the wake of a failure that took their time, disrupted their other work, and created additional stresses, people will become more skeptical and change resistant in the future.

It would be nice if all these questions could be answered and amalgamated with total clarity and certainty. They cannot. Judgment is required. Such is the nature of much that has to do with leadership. Nevertheless, these questions can serve as a useful roadmap.

On more than a few occasions, I have seen a leader, or a group of executives, address these questions and conclude that what appears to be a strategic initiative of a magnitude that they have handled well many times before is in fact significantly different. In some cases, that one judgment has been the single most important decision made that year.

I have also seen groups that found that even their best answers to these questions still left them uncertain about whether they had crossed the line into new territory. That raises an obvious follow-up question: is it better to assume you have crossed the line, or are in the process of doing so, or to assume you are still living in the slower and more stable world of the past?

ABOUT THE AUTHOR

JOHN P. KOTTER is a *New York Times* best-selling author, award-winning business and management thought leader, business entrepreneur, inspirational speaker, and Harvard professor.

Professor Kotter became a member of the Harvard Business School faculty in 1972. By 1980, at the age of 33, he was given tenure and a full professorship— the youngest person ever to have received that award at the Business School. Over the past thirty years, his articles in *Harvard Business Review* have sold millions of reprints. Most recently, his HBR article "Accelerate!" won the 2012 McKinsey Award for the world's most practical and groundbreaking thinking in the business/ management arena.

Dr. Kotter has authored nineteen books to date— twelve of them best sellers. Arguably his most popular book, *Our Iceberg Is Melting,* was published in 2006. This *New York Times* best seller introduced a broad audience to the eight-step philosophy behind Kotter International. Other widely read books include *A Sense of Urgency, The Heart of Change,* and *Leading Change,* which *Time* magazine selected in 2011 as one of the twenty-five most influential business management books ever written.

To supplement his books and expand on his ideas, Dr. Kotter has released several videos on his teachings, most of which are accessible via YouTube. His *Succeeding in a Changing World* was named Best Video Training Product of the Year by *Training Media Review* and also won a Telly Award.

Helping launch Kotter International—a new breed of fast-growing strategy consultants built upon his award-winning work—has been his biggest endeavor in decades.

Professor Kotter is a proud father of two and resides in Cambridge, Massachusetts, with his wife Nancy Dearman.

For more on John Kotter's work and Kotter International please visit www.kotterinternational.com.